Southern Living GARDEN G

Vegetables

Series Editor: Lois Trigg Chaplin

Text by Jennifer Greer

Oxmoor
House.

Contents

Q635 SOU

Library of Congress Catalog Number: 96-67715
ISBN: 0-8487-2245-0
Manufactured in the United States of America
First Printing 1996

Editor-in-Chief: Nancy Fitzpatrick Wyatt
Editorial Director, Special Interest Publications:
Ann H. Harvey
Senior Editor, Editorial Services: Olivia Kindig Wells
Art Director: James Boone

Southern Living Garden Guide VEGETABLES

Series Editor: Lois Trigg Chaplin
Assistant Editor: Kelly Hooper Troiano
Copy Editors: Jennifer K. Mathews,
Anne S. Dickson
Editorial Assistant: Laura A. Fredericks
Garden Editor, *Southern Living*: Linda C. Askey
Indexer: Katharine R. Wiencke
Concept Designer: Eleanor Cameron
Designer: Carol Loria
Senior Photographer, *Southern Living*: Van Chaplin
Production and Distribution Director: Phillip Lee
Associate Production Manager: Vanessa Richardson
Production Coordinator: Marianne Jordan Wilson
Production Assistant: Valerie L. Heard

Our appreciation to the staff of *Southern Living*
magazine for their contributions to this book.

Peppers

Okra blossom

Cover: *Summer vegetables*
Frontispiece: *Leaf lettuce*

Tiger Baby Hybrid Watermelon

Vegetable Primer

The best vegetables you will ever eat are those you have grown in your own garden.

Eggplant is a staple of the summer garden.

A vegetable garden can be easy or challenging, elegant or humble, but it will always be rewarding. Anyone who has eaten fresh sweet corn from the garden, given garden gifts such as gourmet pickles, or grown cherry tomatoes with their children knows the fun and satisfaction of vegetable gardening.

In many regions, vegetables can be grown three or four seasons of the year. *Warm-weather* vegetables, such as tomatoes, grow in summer. *Cool-weather* vegetables, turnips being an example, may be harvested in early spring and fall and withstand frosts. Gardeners can extend their vegetable gardening season so that they have fresh additions on the menu as often as they like.

In vegetable gardening, sun, soil, and water are the three most important ingredients for success. However, there are several other things you can do over which you have more control:

Tomatoes are the most popular of all vegetables to grow.

- choose selections that are adapted to your region
- practice good gardening habits
- use proper tools and equipment
- identify and control pests.

Beginning gardeners often try to garden "by formula," looking for exact combinations of instructions for fertilizing, watering, pest control, and other activities. But veteran gardeners know there are many variables in soil, climate, pests, and other conditions that make it impossible to prescribe formulas for each garden. A simpler and more successful approach is to learn the basics of what makes vegetables grow, experiment with a selection you like, and take note of what works for you in your garden.

The most surprising thing about growing vegetables is how quickly they develop. Many crops grow from tiny seeds to a full harvest within two months. But unlike flowers, vegetables cannot be ignored. Overgrown zucchini will reach the size of a baseball bat, and overmature okra will have the texture of cardboard. A vegetable garden has to be checked daily for water needs and pests. What you see, do, and learn in those regular visits is as rewarding as the harvest.

Designing and Building Your Garden

However large your garden is, it should provide ideal growing conditions for vegetables. And it should be well defined, with a design that complements the house and existing plantings. A garden that fits comfortably into the landscape is pleasing to the eye.

Garden Placement

The first question to ask is: Where should the garden be? There are more options than you may think. Your vegetable garden can be in a charming picket fence inside the front yard. It can be an "edible landscape" that includes lettuce edging a walkway. Or it can be a working garden screened from view.

Choose a Sunny Location

Sunshine is the single most important factor in deciding where to put a garden. A vegetable garden needs at least six hours of sunlight each day. Vegetables planted in the shade are less vigorous, less productive, and may be more susceptible to disease and insect damage than those planted in full sun.

Be careful not to put the garden too close to the house, which will cast shadows; keep planting areas at least 10 feet away from the walls. The north side of the house is not a good location unless the garden is far enough from the house to be out of its shadow. On small lots the best place is usually the south side of the house, since this area receives more sun than any other part of the landscape. The second choice should be the east or west side of the house. If there are no neighboring trees or houses to cast shadows, either location will receive enough sun for a vegetable garden.

If you do not have full sun, consider removing a tree or two. Fruiting crops, such as tomatoes and squash, prefer eight hours of sun, while leafy crops, such as lettuce, can get by with six or even four hours of sun.

A garden in full view of passersby can be a showpiece. Keep it neat, organized, and well tended.

A vegetable garden can be pretty, practical, and productive. It might be the most prominent feature in your landscape or perhaps just a small corner of the backyard.

Lettuce is ideal for edging a sunny brick path. Other ornamental vegetables such as carrots and peppers may also be planted in existing flower beds.

Leafy greens, such as these cool-weather collards, are so ornamental that they can be integrated into an edible landscape in public view.

In Public or Private View

Every landscape has three types of areas: public, private, and service. The public area can be seen from the street; it is typically the front yard. If this area offers the best sunlight, you may decide to place your garden here. It also requires more design consideration and regular attention.

If you want your garden to be in a private location, place it inside a courtyard wall or behind a fence or house. Place it where you can see it from inside the house or near an area where you cook out and entertain.

You may want to screen your garden from view by placing it in the service area of your landscape. A growing bed can be left without an edging and the compost pile can be out in the open. In the service area, you can keep the garden neat enough for maintaining it without worrying about its overall appearance.

If you screen the garden from view, be sure to use a style of fencing that allows air to circulate. Or select shrubs such as yaupon holly that are thin enough for air movement but thick enough to screen. Good air circulation is a must for healthy plants.

Vegetable crops can be attractive additions to private areas of the landscape. An intensive planting of okra adds height and mass to a formal garden.

Convenient and Accessible

Two other location criteria are convenience and accessibility. A garden that is "out of sight, out of mind" can cost you a harvest. Make it convenient so that you can tend it easily and admire your work.

Access is critical. You may need to bring in topsoil or maneuver tillers or other equipment. Plan ahead by leaving wide gates and entryways for vehicles. The garden should also be convenient to the areas where you keep fertilizer, mulch, compost, tools, and equipment.

Also bear in mind that utility companies often run their lines underground, and disturbing an underground line can be costly and dangerous. Utility companies will generally locate and stake out underground lines free of charge if you tell them that you are digging a garden. If you do not notify them, they will hold you responsible for any damage. A septic tank and its drain field should also be located in advance, since pipes could obstruct digging.

Ideal Growing Conditions

In addition to sunlight and good air circulation, vegetables need good drainage, loose soil, and a nearby source of water.

Good Drainage and Level Ground

Surface drainage is as important to vegetables as sunlight. On sites with too little slope, the soil may stay soggy, and seeds and plant roots will rot. On a slope that is too steep, runoff will wash seeds away. A gentle slope with easily crumbled soil, little erosion, and no standing water is ideal.

If your land slopes enough to drain well but erodes or is too steep for comfort while working, plan to terrace the garden. Terracing creates several tiers across the slope, providing deep, well-drained, level areas for the planting beds. The soil is held in place by low retaining walls made from landscape timbers, concrete blocks, stones, or other durable landscape materials.

On a gentle slope that is subject to washing only when rains are heavy, terracing is helpful but not necessary. Plant your crops across the slope, rather than down the hillside, to slow runoff, and mulch with a 3-inch layer of pine straw or hay. You can also garden on a slope by building a set of terraces that creates a series of level beds.

If the property is relatively flat, too little drainage could be a problem. The simplest solution is to build raised beds. (For more about building raised beds see page 12.)

(For more about building raised beds see page 12.)

On a sloping site, terraces create level ground for neat raised beds and intensive plantings.

These raised beds solve drainage problems and are narrow enough for easy reach into the middle from either side. Paths are wide enough for moving garden equipment, and the gravel surface lets water drain.

Loose, Rich Soil

The soil in a vegetable garden needs to be rich, loose, and well drained. Unlike some ornamental plants, vegetables will not grow well in heavy, soggy soil. If your soil is dense clay, you may need to build raised beds and bring topsoil in to fill them or else dig deeply and amend the clay with sand and organic matter. Improving your soil from the start will improve drainage, resulting in healthier plants and higher yields.

Avoid Tree Roots

Roots from a shade tree make a site hard to garden. They interfere with digging and compete with vegetables for valuable nutrients and moisture. The root system of a mature shade tree may extend two or three times the width of the tree canopy. While the tree might survive the loss of a few roots to make room for a garden, cutting a large section of the root system could weaken or kill the tree. Whenever possible, locate your garden away from large trees.

Nearby Source of Water

For the most productive garden, be sure that watering will take as little effort as possible. It is the most frequent maintenance task. If the garden is located far from the water source, it makes sense to install a spigot on the site. (See page 43 for information on sprinklers, drip irrigation, and hoses.)

Another alternative is an underground irrigation system. A contractor can design a system to fit your gardening needs and can specify the valves, sprinkler heads, piping, and controls that your site will require. A do-it-yourself system is often more economical and works equally well when properly installed. Be sure to put in the irrigation system before you begin garden construction.

Watering is the most frequent maintenance chore, so locate your garden near a source of water. Having water within easy reach also helps with seed starting, potting, and planting.

Easy Access to Equipment

When you choose the garden site, remember that you will need a convenient, dry place to store tools, fertilizer, and equipment near the garden. If you do not already have a storage area close by, add a shed or tool house to your garden. The structure can become an attractive addition to the landscape. Try to place it on the north side to avoid shading the garden.

Also consider the location of your compost bin. It should be close to both the garden and the kitchen and should be screened from view. (See pages 28–29 for more on composting.)

Choose Your Garden Style

After you choose a site for your garden, it is time to design the layout. Vegetable gardens have developed a broad range of styles over the years. There are cottage gardens that are planted in small square plots with tidy edges and paths, framed by white picket fences. French parterre gardens have neatly clipped hedges that define the beds and carefully placed red clay pots brimming with herbs and flowers. New American gardens merge vegetables with flowers and use natural materials such as stone and tree limbs in construction. And there are country gardens, where sunflowers, whirligigs, and scarecrows create colorful rural vignettes.

A KITCHEN GARDEN

If you are an avid gardener, you may want to plant two gardens. Try a small garden just outside the kitchen door for vegetables such as peppers, lettuce, and gourmet salad greens; also add a single tomato plant. This handy garden might also include herbs. Place a large garden for more tomatoes, peppers, and larger crops elsewhere, perhaps in the service area.

Measuring 26 x 12 feet, this suburban garden is both attractive and productive.

A small raised bed yields fresh salad greens with a minimum of care.

The Best Size for the Garden

In any garden, size and shape are key considerations. You need to consider four things when deciding on size: the garden's purpose, the amount of time you have to work in it, the amount of space available, and your gardening experience.

If saving money on grocery bills is the objective, plan a large garden that produces year-round. If all you want are fresh salad ingredients, you need only a few feet. You can plant lettuce, scallions, and radishes among flowers. If the time you can spend in the garden is limited, consider a small garden with raised beds or containers where plants can be easily watered. (See page 16 for more information on container gardening and pages 23–25 for tips for increased yield in small gardens.)

A series of backyard beds makes for a large garden that is convenient and produces year-round.

An Appropriate Shape for the Garden

The shape of a garden is often dictated by the lay of the land. Although most people make their gardens rectangular, an L-shaped, triangular, or tiered garden may work better.

A rectangular garden lends itself to neatly organized paths and beds. But on a sloping site, a garden that sweeps across the slope may be more suitable. By bending the garden around a hillside, you will minimize erosion and save garden soil.

The L shape is suitable for many lots, dividing the garden into distinct areas. For instance, you might plant perennial vegetables and herbs in one leg of the L and seasonal vegetables in the other.

The triangular garden adds a dynamic look to the landscape and may be tucked into a corner at the back of the property or in the angle of an L-shaped house.

Changing Character of the Vegetable Garden

Unlike trees or other permanent plantings, your vegetable garden will evolve as your experience increases and you develop a personal style. Design with this in mind. The character of the garden changes from year to year as you rotate crops, choose new selections, and decide on new themes that suit your cooking preferences. Themed gardens may be French or Italian, Southwestern, Oriental, or Native American, or they may be heirloom gardens, gift gardens (full of vegetables for preserving), or gourmet salad gardens.

Permanent Features

It takes work to install and construct permanent features, such as beds, paths, retaining walls, fences, trellises, and underground irrigation. You need to be sure that they are properly placed, designed, and built—in keeping with the overall style of the garden.

Design of Beds

The most efficient garden devotes a maximum area to beds and a minimum area to paths. Determine bed width by the length of your reach; you should be able to reach comfortably to the center of the bed from either side. For most people, this means a bed width of 4 to 5 feet. Beds that are narrower use garden space less efficiently.

Plan the size of the beds in a simple-to-figure number of square feet. For example, beds 5 feet wide by 20 feet long total 100 square feet. It is easy to determine how much fertilizer or mulch you will need for beds this size because package recommendations are easier to calculate on a 100-square-foot basis.

Triangular garden beds take advantage of space you might not think was usable. Brick paving and edging, along with landscape timbers, form attractive permanent beds.

The most efficient garden devotes a maximum area to beds and a minimum area to paths. This simple design makes it easy to plant, maintain, and harvest vegetables.

Raised beds improve drainage and create a neat, well-defined garden layout.

Raised Beds

You may build raised beds with brick, landscape timbers, rot-resistant lumber, railroad ties, or concrete blocks. Landscape timbers are 4 x 4s of treated lumber sold specifically for bed building. Raising beds as high as 1 to 3 feet reduces the distance you have to stoop. One disadvantage to permanent, hard edgings is that you will need to hand-turn the soil rather than use a tiller.

Here are a few pointers for working with materials popular for building raised beds.

• **Wood.** Whether you use landscape timbers or dimensional lumber (2 x 4, 2 x 6, for example), be sure it is pressure treated for ground contact or is a rot-resistant type. Make certain the wood has not been treated with a preservative that is toxic to plants, such as creosote. Avoid using lumber that is only 1 inch thick; it will warp under the strain of supporting soil. Anchor lumber firmly into the ground with stakes that are driven at least 18 inches deep and no more than 4 feet apart for maximum strength. Miter corners and nail in both directions, as you would a picture frame.

• **Railroad ties.** Use only old, weathered ties, as much of the toxic creosote will have leached out. A single layer does not need staking for support, but each tie should be sunk into the ground 1 or 2 inches. To stack ties, bore holes through them with an industrial drill. Drive sections of galvanized pipe through the holes into the ground with a sledgehammer; overlap corners of stacked ties for strength. Cut ties with a chain saw; (wear safety goggles and ear protection, and watch out for nails).

• **Concrete blocks.** Filled with earth, concrete blocks in a single line or level row make a sturdy edging. They are also a good place to grow herbs, which benefit from the lime that leaches from the blocks. Stacked blocks must be mortared to form a stable, permanent edging.

• **Bricks.** A single row of bricks set on end is fairly easy to install and makes an attractive, inexpensive edging. If stacked, the bricks must be mortared. If you choose bricks for building raised beds, be sure to order a grade that will withstand weathering.

Paths

No matter what size beds you have, you must have a convenient way to get to the crops. Permanent pathways separate beds and steer garden traffic around the beds so that the soil does not become compacted.

Width is the key consideration in designing garden paths. Major paths that lead into and out of the garden should be wide enough to handle a garden cart, wheelbarrow, or wheelchair; 3 feet is the minimum, but 4 feet is better. Other paths between rows and beds may be as narrow as 18 inches.

There are many suitable materials for pathways: mulch, brick, gravel, concrete stepping pads, stone, and railroad ties. (Space stepping pads no more than 2 to 3 inches apart so that you can easily push a wheelbarrow over the path.) The most simple, inexpensive, and practical path is of pine straw, hay, or bark.

Permanent pathways separate beds, handle garden traffic, and anchor the overall design.

BUILDING AN ENABLING GARDEN

People who suffer from aches and pains, who do not like to stoop, or who use a wheelchair can work in a garden if it is designed correctly. Try some of the following suggestions:
• Build beds 2 to 3 feet high so that they can be worked easily from a wheelchair; beds that are 3 feet high can be worked while standing. Make beds only about 2 feet wide unless they can be reached from both sides.
• Add 12-inch-wide rims to the tops of beds for sitting on; 24 inches is a comfortable seating height.
• Locate the garden on level ground, or use ramps instead of steps on a gentle slope. Make paths 4 feet wide and hard-surfaced to accommodate wheelchairs.
• Buy light, foam-grip tools and store them within easy reach.
• Design a watering system that is automatic or that is simple to turn on and off.

Beds that are about 2 feet high and that feature wide rims for sitting can be worked easily. They are also good for gardeners who use wheelchairs.

Fences create privacy for a garden while defining and framing it. They also protect plantings from rabbits, dogs, and other large animals.

Trellises, Fences, and Sheds

An advantage to having permanent beds is that structures such as trellises, fences, and sheds can be permanent as well. You can build them out of durable materials such as pressure-treated pine, redwood, cypress, cedar, or even synthetic materials.

• **Trellises.** You may want to install permanent trellises to avoid having to erect them every year. However, you will have to pay special attention to rotating crops such as pole beans, English peas, and cucumbers to prevent diseases that can build up in the soil. Be careful not to place the trellis where it will shade other vegetables. Also, do not let the trellis block your view of the garden from indoors; rather, use it to screen your garden from your neighbors. (See page 44 for more information.)

• **Fences.** These can perform a variety of functions. They keep rabbits, dogs, and other large animals out of the garden. Fences can double as a trellis or support for vining crops while setting off the design of the garden and serving as a backdrop for the vegetables. They also provide privacy. When choosing from the many fence styles, consider the shadows they may cast, and be sure that the designs are open enough to allow good air circulation.

• **Sheds.** If you do not already have a shed, you may decide to build one for handy access to gardening tools, equipment, and supplies. A shed can be a showpiece in a vegetable garden, so leave plenty of room for it, preferably on the north side of the garden. Place it where it will not cast a shadow on your crops.

TIPS FOR A CHILDREN'S GARDEN

• Allow children to grow whatever they choose. Give them a small section of the garden that they can tend themselves.

• Start with transplants that grow quickly, such as cherry tomatoes. Mix them with cosmos or other flowers for cutting.

• Plant seeds of fast-growing crops such as radishes or garden cress. For extra fun, plant seeds in a pattern that forms the child's initials. Bean seeds are also good for children to plant; they are large and will germinate quickly. Pole beans grown on a tepee made from long stakes will create an enclosure in which to play.

• Supply young gardeners with well-tilled soil, a sunny location, fresh seeds, and good-quality transplants. Take time to teach proper techniques for planting, thinning, weeding, mulching, and watering.

• Check garden supply stores for tools made for children, or cut down the handles of full-sized implements that are light enough for a child to handle. Be sure to discuss tool safety and care before beginning any work in the garden.

• To help pass the time while waiting for the harvest, plan activities such as making a scarecrow or watching the bees pollinate the squash. Teach children about beneficial insects such as the parsleyworm, which turns into a graceful black swallowtail butterfly. Older children can also take photographs of the garden and keep garden diaries.

Give children their own space in the garden. To make their gardening experience a success, have them start with good soil and easy, fast-growing plants.

15

Growing Vegetables in Containers

Leaf lettuce is one of the easiest vegetables to grow in containers.

Vegetables in containers need more care than those drawing sun, water, and nutrients in a garden plot.

There are, however, many vegetables that will grow as well in containers as they do in the ground if you provide proper placement, water, and nutrition. Containers may be necessary if the only sunny spot you have is a patio, a deck, or an entryway or if your soil is too poor or pest-infested for vegetables to grow well. If you want to interest children in gardening or you are unable to maintain a large garden, containers may be a good choice for you.

Select Large Containers

To avoid stress on the vegetables from heat and drought, choose containers that hold at least five gallons of soil. The shape of a container is also important. Wide, shallow, boatlike dishes are fine for crops like leaf lettuce, but the soil will dry out quickly. Root crops demand pots that are at least 1 inch deeper than the anticipated length of the root. Large, leafy plants, such as bush squash or tomatoes, need a pot that is deep and wide; an 18-inch pot is a minimum to accommodate a good root system and to hold enough water for steady growth.

Good Potting Mix Is Crucial

Always use a premium-quality commercial potting mix to fill containers. Garden soil is not suited for pots; it is too heavy and may carry diseases and weed seeds. A premium mix is sterile, lightweight, and well drained, yet able to hold moisture and nutrients. Look for mixes that specify contents and include quality ingredients such as sphagnum peat moss, composted bark, vermiculite, perlite, or sand. A good mix is pH balanced so there is no need to add lime. Premium-quality mixes will lose their structure within a year in warm, humid climates but may last two years in cooler climates. Avoid bagged topsoil or inexpensive mixes that do not list ingredients.

You will also find lightweight mixes specially designed for starting seeds. While these are excellent for starting your own transplants, they are too lightweight to support full-sized plants. They will also break down quickly and pack down too hard within a season.

A POTTING SOIL RECIPE

If you have several pots to fill, it is more economical to mix your own potting soil. Use a 3-gallon bucket to fill a 3-cubic-foot wheelbarrow for this basic mix:

1 bucket sphagnum peat moss
1 bucket coarse sand
1 bucket finely ground bark
2 cups lime
1/3 pound iron sulfate
2 pounds slow-release vegetable food or 6 pounds cottonseed meal

A coffee filter in the pot will prevent soil from washing through the drainage hole.

Planting and Care

To plant in a container, cover the drainage hole with a piece of window screen or mesh or with a coffee filter. This lets excess water drain and keeps the soil from leaking out. Fill containers to within 1 inch of the top and plant seeds or transplants as you would in the ground. In boxes or pots, be sure to plant rows of vegetables at the proper spacing.

Vegetables grown in containers need watering every day in sunny, hot weather but less often during cool, damp periods in spring and fall. When the soil surface is dry to a depth of ½ inch, water the plants with a watering can or a hose with a nozzle attached to create a fine spray. Because water is so important, you may want to set up a drip system and a simple timer on the outdoor spigot to do the work for you. (See page 43 for more about drip systems.)

Frequent watering washes the fertilizer out of the soil more quickly, so you will also need to supplement with a soluble fertilizer. Use a soluble fertilizer diluted to one-fifth the amount recommended on the label and apply every other time you water.

Vegetables in pots are more sensitive to changes in air temperature than vegetables planted in the ground. In spring and summer, you can expect the plants to grow more rapidly. In fall or winter, the soil in containers will probably freeze before the ground does and even hardy plants, such as broccoli or collards, will wilt because the available water is frozen. When a hard or prolonged freeze is predicted, you may have to bury containers in a mound of pine straw, or harvest the vegetables.

Best Bets for Container Gardening

You can harvest a surprising number of vegetables from a container garden. Nematodes and soilborne diseases are not a problem. Dwarf or bush selections are often as productive as full-sized versions.

Here are some "best bets" for container gardening: bush beans, beets, broccoli, cabbage, short and medium carrots, Swiss chard, bush cucumbers, eggplant, leaf lettuce, onions (use as scallions), bush peas, peppers, potatoes, radishes, spinach, bush tomatoes, and turnips.

GOURMET BOUQUETS

If you like to grow vegetables for fun, plant them in hanging baskets or tabletop pots. You will not get a bountiful harvest, but you will receive a lot of compliments. Try parsley and marigolds in summer or lettuce, onions, and pansies in spring or fall. Remember to water hanging baskets daily during warm weather. You may also grow vegetables in small containers as a short-lived centerpiece for a party or other special occasion.

A cone-shaped frame allows you to grow vining plants, such as cucumbers, in a large pot.

Planning Your Garden

How well you plan your vegetable garden determines how successful it will be and how much enjoyment you will derive from it.

Radishes, turnip greens, and broccoli thrive in cool weather.

Start with a good written plan for each season to increase productivity and minimize problems. After the harvest, the plan becomes a historical record of what does or does not grow well in your garden, as well as a guide for rotating crops the following year.

Planning and Timing for Each Season

Many people associate a vegetable garden with only spring and summer, but veteran gardeners also grow an array of vegetables during fall and winter. Fall is best for many crops including leafy greens, broccoli, and carrots. Alternating cool- and warm-weather vegetables allows you to harvest fresh vegetables nearly year-round.

Cool-Weather Vegetables

Cool-weather vegetables grow best in spring and fall; some also grow in winter in areas where daytime temperatures are 40 to 60 degrees and nights are rarely below freezing. Some cool-weather vegetables include lettuce, potatoes, carrots, radishes, gourmet greens, broccoli, cauliflower, cabbage, kale, mustard, onions, green peas, beets, and turnips. These vegetables do not grow in the heat. A cool-weather perennial vegetable, such as asparagus, tolerates summer but grows and produces in the spring months.

Warm-Weather Vegetables

Warm-weather vegetables thrive in the warm temperatures of late spring and summer. These vegetables include corn, beans, cucumbers, eggplant, peppers, sweet potatoes, pumpkins, summer squash, melons, tomatoes, and Southern peas. Warm-weather crops will be killed by fall frost.

Keeping the Garden Going

For a garden that produces year-round, plan for the summer and fall gardens that will follow your spring garden. For example, when spring cabbage is harvested, what will replace it for summer? Bush beans are one possibility. And when the beans finish producing, what

Warm-weather vegetables will be at their peak in midsummer.

can you grow in that same spot in fall? Spinach is a good choice. This planting of one crop followed by another is called *succession planting.* Another good succession planting is carrots (spring), tomatoes (summer), and collards and kale (fall).

Timing is critical to the garden's progress. When it is time to plant beans, corn, okra, peppers, and squash, much of the garden may still be occupied by cool-weather vegetables such as broccoli, cabbage, collards, and lettuce. In this case, you need to know which vegetables you can delay planting until space is available. For example, plant squash as early as possible after the last spring frost, before squash vine borers become numerous. Likewise, transplants such as peppers and tomatoes should be planted at the earliest safe date to minimize the time they stay in flats. These young transplants may be set in gaps created by the harvesting of lettuce or other cool-weather vegetables in the garden.

Heat-tolerant vegetables started from seed (beans, corn, melons, okra, and Southern peas) can wait a few weeks.

Rotating Crops

Ideally, you should change the location of each vegetable in your garden every year. This allows you to stay one step ahead of insects such as sweet potato weevils that build up in the soil, and it gives the soil a chance to replenish nutrients lost to a particular vegetable. Do not plant the same vegetable or a member of the same vegetable family in the same row or section of the garden for three or four years. For example, potatoes and peppers are in the same family and should not be planted one after the other.

In gardens where the amount of space and sun exposure makes it difficult to move crops around, skip a year planting a crop if a soilborne problem develops.

Plan for a succession of crops by planting tomato transplants (for summer crops) in among spring leaf lettuce, which will be harvested shortly.

When space allows, design the garden so that it is easy to rotate vegetables to different beds each year.

VEGETABLE FAMILIES

Be sure to rotate plants in these vegetable families each year:

• Broccoli, cabbage, cauliflower, collards, kale
• Lettuce, spinach
• Cucumbers, melons, pumpkins, squash
• Beans, peas
• Eggplant, peppers, potatoes, tomatoes
• Beets, Swiss chard
• Mustard greens, turnips

19

Cabbage provides only one harvest, so plant an early-maturing selection in spring to free the space for a summer vegetable.

Dwarf okra is one of the most productive of all summer vegetables.

The Best Use of Time and Space

Smart gardeners maximize the time that the garden is productive by using three strategies. While just one of these alone will make your garden more productive, combining all three will yield the most bountiful harvest. There are also other ways to maximize the harvest, but the strategies that follow apply to garden layout. Techniques, such as interplanting, are discussed later.

• **Use early-maturing selections.** Selections that mature quickly need less time in the garden because their life cycles are short. Those that provide only one harvest, such as cabbage or cauliflower, can be replaced as soon as they have been harvested.

• **Stagger maturity dates.** You can also extend the harvest by planting early-, mid-, and late-season selections of the same vegetable. By staggering the plantings you can avoid having more corn than you can use one week and no harvest at all the next. To prevent overlapping, wait two to three weeks between plantings of different selections.

• **Make repeated plantings.** Another way to extend the harvest is to make repeated plantings of the same selection. If the only selection of sweet corn you like is a late-season type, such as Silver Queen, you can sow part of the crop on the earliest possible date and then make a second planting when the first corn has three or four leaves. Continue planting at this interval until midsummer. You can stagger plantings of cabbage, squash, and tomatoes in a similar manner.

Repeated plantings are especially useful for crops such as radishes, beans, and lettuce, which you may use frequently in food preparation but in small quantities.

Always be ready to replant. If tomatoes follow onions on your garden plan, be sure you have tomato transplants on hand the day you harvest the onions. This way you never have an idle space. To be sure you have seeds or transplants when you need them, plan ahead. Order enough seeds for continuous planting, and be prepared to grow your own transplants for planting in the summer.

Reasons for Selecting Certain Vegetables

Deciding what to plant depends on the overall purpose of your garden. The following are examples of what you might consider when choosing vegetable selections.

• **Economy.** If your goal is to spend less on groceries, choose vegetables that are expensive to buy at the supermarket, such as asparagus, along with those that are most productive, such as tomatoes, squash, and okra. Also select vegetables that may be frozen or canned so that you can avoid paying high prices at the store when they are out of season.

• **Small gardens.** Plant vegetables that are highly productive and space efficient; in other words, you want to plant those having a high total yield per square foot and a short planting-to-harvest time. Here are some good choices: beans, lima beans (pole type), beets, broccoli, carrots, cucumbers (on supports), leaf lettuce, mustard, green bunching onions, edible podded peas, sweet peppers, radishes, spinach, summer squash, Swiss chard, tomatoes (on supports), turnips, and zucchini.

Corn and sweet potatoes as well as vining selections of pumpkins and winter squash require too much space for small gardens.

• **Extended harvests.** Some vegetables produce for many months. Collards, kale, and spinach, for example, are extremely hardy, surviving fall and winter freezes. If properly cared for, a single planting of pole beans and vining tomatoes will produce until the first frost.

Collards and other hardy greens stand in the garden through fall and winter freezes until you are ready to harvest them.

KEEP A GARDENING RECORD

A record of your activities provides a written account of each season's successes and failures. Next year, this information will eliminate guesswork.

The first step in record keeping is to label each plant or row with the name of the selection and the date planted. Then you can identify and record the performance of each plant.

Write your observations in a notebook. Keep each season's plan there as well, to aid you with crop rotation the following year. Here are some other things you will want to note:

• Whether you start from seeds or transplants, the planting date, the date each selection began bearing, and when production stopped. This information will help you plan for successive harvests next year.

• Disease resistance; problems with heat or cold; and the fruit size, yield, flavor, and texture of each selection. If you are trying several selections of a vegetable, this will allow you to make comparisons.

• The date of insect and disease outbreaks in your garden. This will help you anticipate their occurrence next year. In the case of devastating foliage diseases that appear every year, such as early blight and late blight of tomatoes, you can often prevent infection by spraying just before the time the disease usually appears.

• **Flavor and freshness.** These usually are the primary reasons for growing vegetables. Although corn does not produce much in proportion to the amount of space it requires, it is impossible to buy corn as good as the fresh ears that come directly from your garden. For that reason alone, many gardeners find a place for it. The same is true of tomatoes and eggplant.

• **Ease.** Beginners may want to choose the crops that are easiest to grow. Consider beans, cabbage, collards, cucumbers, cress, hot peppers, kale, leaf lettuce, mustard, green onions, Southern peas, radishes, summer squash, Swiss chard, cherry tomatoes, and turnips.

Layout of Plants

A large part of planning involves deciding how to arrange the vegetables in the garden so that they grow well, produce the amounts you need, and are easy to maintain and harvest.

If the garden is on a slope, the rows or beds should run across the slope to reduce erosion. To capture the most sunlight in the summer, track the sun's path and lay the rows from east to west.

For an attractive garden that allows for more of one crop and less of another, consider laying out the garden in a square with rows on the diagonal. The rows in the center will be the longest and rows to each side will be proportionally shorter.

Draw a Diagram of the Garden

Experienced gardeners often start with a written plan. It does not have to be fancy, although some gardeners use a computer so they can update the plan easily. You need a neat, legible plan that shows planting dates, where each vegetable goes, and which way the rows or beds will run.

A scale drawing of your garden also will help you avoid mistakes. Plot the location of each vegetable on the diagram, and follow it.

First, measure off the dimensions of your garden and draw your diagram to scale on graph paper.

Fill in rows and beds by designating areas for each vegetable. Draw the permanent beds for any perennial crops or flowers that you are using to add

A plan makes laying out the garden much easier. Decide ahead of time where to plant each vegetable, keeping in mind placement techniques like planting on the diagonal.

color to the garden. Then add tall crops, such as trellised English peas or corn. Be sure to plant taller vegetables toward the north end or along the edge of the garden so they do not shade shorter vegetables. Then group the rest of the vegetables according to like planting times and harvest dates.

Planting To Increase Yield

There are several things you can do to help increase the yield from each square foot of garden. Planting in wide rows, making use of a trellis whenever possible, and planting vegetables so they quickly follow or even overlap previous crops in the growing season are three easy ways to get more from your garden.

Traditionally, vegetables are planted in a single row, with an aisle or path between each row. The disadvantage of single rows is that much of your space is devoted to paths instead of vegetables, and the bare ground requires maintenance.

A better method is to plant suitable vegetables in wide rows or beds. Rows may be from 1½ to 2 feet wide; beds may be up to 6 feet wide. Determine a comfortable width; you should be able to reach the middle easily. Wide rows increase productivity because more space is available for growing vegetables. Because plants in a wide row are spaced more closely than they are in single rows, each plant may yield less than it might in a single row. However, the increased number of plants in the wide row more than makes up for the difference, for the yield is two to four times greater than that of a garden laid out in single rows. Maintenance is also reduced, since denser planting tends to crowd out weeds.

Planting in Square-Foot Beds

Another popular layout uses square beds. It calls for laying out a 4-foot-by-4-foot bed and dividing it into a grid of 16 sections, each measuring 1 square foot. The beds look like a quilt at harvesttime and they offer high yields in small spaces. You can plant different crops from square to square or plant the same vegetable in each one. For example, in the spring, a 1-foot-by-1-foot square might hold 4 leaf lettuce plants, 12 carrots, or 1 broccoli plant. In the summer, each square could support 1 plant of squash, corn, or okra, for a total of 16 plants—the equivalent of one whole row in the garden.

The use of beds or blocks produces high yields in small spaces. You can plant different crops from square to square or the same vegetable in each square.

Conserve space by planting fast-maturing vegetables, such as lettuce, under or alongside taller, slow-maturing ones, such as broccoli.

Plant Two Vegetables in One Space

Low-growing vegetables such as lettuce, spinach, and radishes, which mature in a short time, will grow beneath and between crops such as broccoli and cabbage, which stand in the garden longer. This technique is called ***interplanting.***

Be sure the vegetables you interplant have compatible growth habits so that they do not compete with or crowd each other. For example, broccoli grows tall while lettuce stays low (and benefits from the shade). Similarly, tomato transplants may be planted alongside cabbage. Interplanting is also useful when many cool-weather vegetables are still in the ground at the time warm-weather crops are planted. Other popular combinations include parsley with tomatoes, dill with cabbage, lettuce with onions, and spinach with broccoli or collards. Experience will suggest even more combinations of plants for your garden.

Other Techniques That Increase Yield

The techniques of planting in wide rows or squares, planting in succession, and interplanting help you get more from your garden. Here are some other techniques:

• Enhance the soil with compost and other organic matter for maximum fertility and deep rooting.

• Start with transplants whenever possible. They give you a month's head start on growth, reducing the wait for the first harvest.

• Use trellises for beans, cantaloupe, cucumbers, peas, squash, and tomatoes. When plants grow upward, they require less space. Trellised plants are often more productive also, because the leaves are more exposed to the sun.

Permanent Plantings, Flowers, and Fun

When planning the garden for each season, consider ways to make it attractive and fun as well as functional.

• Plant edible flowers to enhance the garden and the vegetables you prepare. In spring and fall, try cool-weather annuals such as pansies, violas, calendulas, nasturtiums, or ornamental cabbage and kale. Plant edible warm-weather annuals such as Lemon Gem marigolds in summer. Edible perennials include the blossoms of daylilies.

• Incorporate flowers for cutting, such as cosmos, daisies, sunflowers, and zinnias.

• Consider low-growing shrubs such as sheared boxwood for green borders and accents. Herbs also make good borders; try rosemary or chives.

• In cool weather, edge the garden with leaf lettuce, parsley, or other pretty green vegetables.

• Add features such as potted flowers or herbs, scarecrows, or arbors. Picnic tables, benches, and swings add visual interest and will make the garden a destination.

If you are short on time and space, plant a few vegetables among your flowers in ornamental beds. Lettuce, shown here with pinks, chives, daisies, sweet William, stachys, Johnny-jump-ups, and lamb's-ear, adds bright lime green to a spring border.

Getting Started

Rich loam is essential for roots to grow down deep and bring up air, water, and nutrients.

Starting with good, well-drained soil is key to a productive vegetable garden.

Once you have provided adequate soil, you must choose selections adapted to your area and then grow them from seed or buy healthy transplants.

Soil: The Magic Medium

A vegetable garden is only as good as the soil in which it grows. In loose, fertile soil, plants can send roots deep into the ground to capture air, water, and nutrients. In soils with poor texture and low fertility, root growth is limited.

Always Do a Soil Test

The first step in preparing the soil is to test it to determine the availability of plant nutrients and the pH (acidity or alkalinity) of the soil. The pH is measured on a scale of 1 (pure acid) to 14 (pure alkaline), with 7 being neutral. Vegetables grow best in a pH range of 6.0 to 6.8. In soils that are strongly acid or alkaline, essential nutrients are bound in the soil chemistry.

You can test the soil anytime before planting, but the best time is in late summer or fall. That way, if your soil test results recommend that you add lime or sulfur to change the pH, the amendment will have time to take effect. Test your soil every three years.

These soil testing services are offered to you by the United States Department of Agriculture Cooperative Extension Service through its county offices or your state's land grant university. Less precise do-it-yourself kits are also available.

Changing the pH

If your soil is too acid for vegetables (pH below 5.5), you will need to raise the pH by adding pelletized or powdered lime. The soil test results will tell you how much to add, but it will take three to six months to see the full effect.

Alkaline soil needs sulfur to increase its acidity. Again, look to your soil test for the specific amount. Sulfur is available in several forms. Elemental sulfur can be worked into the soil as a dust or as granules. Wettable sulfur is mixed with water and poured on the soil.

Amending Problem Soil

Gardeners generally start with a soil that is less than ideal. Sandy soil is loose and well drained, but it also is infertile and dries out quickly. Clay soil becomes hard when dry and turns sticky when wet, and although clay retains nutrients well, it drains poorly.

The ideal soil, described as *loam,* is the perfect combination of sand, clay, and *silt* (fine particles) and is rich in organic matter. It sticks together if you squeeze it in your hand but it crumbles readily. Loamy soil retains moisture and nutrients but drains well.

If your soil is thin, rocky, or otherwise difficult to work, consider buying a truckload of good topsoil and starting with that. Good topsoil will be dark and rich in organic matter. Ask local gardeners where to find the best topsoil, or, if you cannot be assured of the quality, buy a truckload of compost instead.

Gather soil from different areas of the garden for testing.

Organic Matter: The Secret Ingredient

You can amend any poor soil with organic matter by working the amendments into the soil in late winter before planting the spring garden and in late summer when you plant the fall garden. Apply at

Most gardeners have to work to improve the soil, amending it with composted leaves, other organic matter, and sand.

27

least a 4-inch layer of organic matter each time, working it into the soil to a depth of 8 to 12 inches. A general, all-purpose recipe for a good garden soil mix is one part organic matter, one part builder's sand, and one part topsoil.

Experienced gardeners add truckloads of organic matter such as compost, leaf mold, or composted bark to the soil to improve drainage and aeration of clay soils and to increase the capability of sandy soils to hold moisture and nutrients. Composted organic matter also contributes nutrients to the soil. Add organic matter each time you plant. It decomposes quickly in hot climates and intensively cultivated gardens.

Always use completely composted material. Bacteria that decompose organic matter use nitrogen and will compete with your vegetables for this essential nutrient.

Good Organic Soil Amendments

• **Leaf mold or composted leaves.** Shredding or chopping leaves with a lawn mower before composting them will speed the process.

• **Well-rotted sawdust.** Local sawmills are often a good source of sawdust, but avoid sawdust from chemically treated lumber. Be sure to compost sawdust; undecomposed sawdust will rob the soil of nitrogen.

• **Pine bark.** Buy pulverized bark in 3-cubic-foot bags or by the truckload. Pulverized pine bark is often sold in bags labeled "soil conditioner." If the bark is not composted, add an extra cup of slow-release fertilizer for every 100 square feet to supply the nitrogen it will need for decomposition.

• **Manure.** Dehydrated, composted cow manure in bags is the most commonly available form of manure. Do not apply fresh manure from local farms or stables to the soil just before planting because it can burn seeds and seedlings and introduce weeds. Work fresh manure into the soil in late fall if planning a spring garden, or compost it with other materials or by itself.

• **Composted kitchen and yard waste.** You can produce a continuous supply of this in a compost bin or compost pile at home. A city may also sell composted leaves and refuse by the truckload.

MAINTAINING HEALTHY SOIL

Once you have good soil, you must work to keep it that way. Here are some tips for keeping the soil loose and replenishing nutrients.

• Use organic mulches, such as shredded leaves, pine bark, pine straw, or compost. See page 39 for more about mulches.

• Rotate crops, as different vegetables take different nutrients out of the soil.

• Cultivate earthworms as partners. They tunnel deep down, aerating the soil for better penetration of water and air. They also excrete "casts" that are rich in the nutrients essential for plants. Before using an insecticide or fungicide, you may wish to call your Extension agent to see if the pesticide is toxic to earthworms.

• Work in 4 inches of organic matter in spring and fall.

Cooking Your Own Compost

Some people buy compost (decayed organic matter) because they do not have a place to make their own. But it is easy and less expensive to make compost at home. And composting cuts down on the amount of household waste sent to landfills.

Good ingredients for compost include cooled wood ashes, kitchen refuse (fruit and vegetable peelings, eggshells, and coffee grounds), and garden waste (leaves, grass clippings, and spent vegetables, herbs, and flowers).

Do not compost meat scraps or grass clippings from a lawn that has been treated with an herbicide or that has gone to seed. Also avoid weeds and plants with insect and disease problems.

To begin, spread an 8-inch-deep layer of organic material on the ground or at the bottom of the cage or bin. Limit the grass clippings and whole leaves used in the compost to a layer no thicker than 2 to 3 inches or they will form an impermeable mat.

Sprinkle this first organic layer with 1 cup of nitrogen fertilizer (such as 10-10-10) per 10 to 15 square feet to aid decomposition. Or apply a 2-inch layer of manure, blood meal, or cottonseed meal. Then add another 8-inch layer of organic matter. Top this with 2 inches of soil to introduce the bacteria that decompose the organic materials, and dust the soil with lime. Lime helps maintain the proper level of acidity for the bacteria. (If you regularly compost wood ashes, reduce the amount of lime you add by one-quarter to one-half.)

Repeat these layers, dampening each layer as you build the pile. Compost needs moisture but should never be allowed to become soggy, as this halts decomposition. If your pile is sheltered from rain or located in the sun, dampen it weekly.

Every four to six weeks, turn the pile with a turning fork to mix the ingredients and introduce air, which is required by the bacteria. A bad odor means the pile needs turning. Move materials from the top and sides of the pile to the center, where they will decompose faster. After a few months, most of the compost should be ready to use. (You can also purchase a barrel-like composter, which turns with a crank of the handle to make this job easier.)

Remember that decomposition is rapid in hot weather; in winter it will be slow. Be aware that compost can catch fire if the heat produced during decomposition becomes intense. Be careful not to apply too much high-nitrogen fertilizer to the pile.

Compost is a rich organic amendment that gardeners call "black gold."

No matter what they are made of, compost bins must be constructed to allow air to get inside.

Preparing the Soil for Planting

The cardinal rule of soil preparation is never to work the soil when it is wet. This is especially critical in clay soil. In soil worked when wet, clods will form that are nearly impossible to break up. To test the soil for moisture, squeeze a fistful into a ball, and then drop it from a height of 3 feet. If the ball crumbles, the soil is dry enough to work.

Composted organic matter, fertilizer, and other materials should be worked into the soil at least two or three days before planting. Use a premium-quality, slow-release vegetable fertilizer for best results; this type of fertilizer will continue feeding plants throughout the season. If you choose organic fertilizers, you will need to apply larger quantities initially and use additional fertilizer throughout the season. See page 37 for more about fertilizing.

Work the soil 8 to 12 inches deep. However, if you have shallow topsoil with poor, heavy subsoil, it is best to bring up not more than 1 or 2 inches of subsoil each year to avoid diluting the good topsoil.

Rich, well-worked soil is a pleasure to plant in.

Choosing Appropriate Selections

The many vegetable selections available today may make choosing what to grow more complicated, but they also make gardening easier. Vegetable breeders have developed plants with increased yields, improved disease resistance, and adaptation to specific climates. These improved plants make your chances for success good.

There are many qualities to consider when choosing vegetable selections, the most critical being adaptability—how well a specific selection grows in your area. A tomato that grows in California may not be resistant to the nematodes and wilt diseases that kill plants in the South. The vegetable profiles beginning on page 48 include many popular selections, but you should always check with local sources such as your county Extension agent.

The way you plan to use a vegetable also influences your decisions. For example, certain tomatoes are better suited to canning; pickling cucumbers are smaller than slicing types; and some onions are better for storage than others.

Plant size and growth habit are especially important in a small garden. Where every square inch counts, you want to maximize yield using the most compact, most highly productive selections. You'll also want to consider the number of days selections will require before they are ready to harvest, especially if you are planting a three- or four-season garden.

Starting from Seeds or Transplants

You will start most vegetables from either seeds or transplants. Vegetables started as transplants often produce sooner than those started from seed. But some vegetables, such as root crops, should be started from seed sown into the garden, or they may be stunted. Starting from seed is also easier and more practical for plants that grow quickly or do not transplant easily. These include beans, beets, carrots, corn, cucumbers, melons, okra, peas, radishes, and squash.

Tips for Purchasing Seed

For the best start, buy fresh seeds from a reputable source. Selections offered locally are usually the established selections for the area, and you should buy early for the best choice.

Mail-order seed catalogs offer more variety and are a good source of information about specific selections. Look for catalogs that come from companies based in your part of the country. Then watch for selections that are disease resistant and slow to **bolt,** or flower (go to seed prematurely). Also look for new hybrids, and *All-America Selections* winners, which have been tested in trial gardens across the country and judged superior. Although an All-America Selections winner may not be equally well adapted to all areas, it is more likely to give you good results than a selection picked at random.

Presoaking and Presprouting Seeds

Some seeds have very hard coats and benefit from being soaked overnight before planting. These include the seeds of beans, melons, okra, and squash. Others, such as sugar snap peas and supersweet corn, benefit from *presprouting,* or being forced to sprout before being planted. To presprout seeds, sprinkle them on a damp paper towel, roll the towel and tuck it inside a plastic bag or wax paper, and place in a warm place such as on top of the refrigerator. In three to five days, the seeds will sprout. Plant them immediately and keep the soil moist for a week.

Starting from Transplants

Starting with transplants is convenient and reduces the time until harvest by a month or more. It is the best way to grow vegetables such as broccoli, cabbage, cauliflower, and onions, which produce only one major harvest, since garden space will then be tied up for the shortest possible time. Tomatoes, eggplant, and peppers started directly from seed take about six weeks longer to begin producing than those started from transplants. Since these vegetables produce for an extended period, you can begin harvesting sooner if you start with transplants.

Buying Transplants

Buy transplants early in the planting season to be sure of getting the best quality. Look for sturdy, compact plants that are a healthy green. A poor transplant is no bargain, no matter what the price. Avoid tall, spindly plants with weak, thin stems and yellow leaves.

Young transplants give the best results. Large plants that are in flower or bearing fruit will lag behind vigorous leafy transplants when set out in the garden.

Also, avoid rootbound transplants. Some healthy, white roots should be visible through holes in the bottom of the pack or flat, but if there are roots growing out of the holes, the plants may be stunted.

Examine the plants closely for leaf spots or other signs of disease. And look for insects, checking the leaf undersides carefully. If you see whiteflies, mites, other pests, or evidence of disease, do not buy the plants.

How To Grow Your Own Transplants

You can grow healthy transplants at home if you maintain the proper temperatures and provide adequate moisture and light. There are many ways to grow transplants, but here is one of the easiest:

• Set up a small seed-starting project in front of a window that faces south or west. Buy a special stand or set up your own on a table or bench with a waterproof surface.

• Supplement the sunlight with fluorescent light; standard fluorescent lights are fine. Hang a 40-watt, cool white fluorescent tube 3 to 6 inches above the trays. You will need an adjustable support that allows you to move the fixture up as the seedlings grow.

STARTING TRANSPLANTS FROM SEEDS

Vegetable	Number of Weeks from Sowing to Transplant Size
Asparagus*	10 - 12
Broccoli	6 - 8
Cabbage	6 - 8
Cauliflower	6 - 8
Collards	6 - 8
Eggplant	6 - 8
Endive, Escarole	6 - 8
Kale	6 - 8
Lettuce**	4 - 6
Onions	8 - 10
Peppers*	6 - 8
Swiss Chard	4
Tomatoes	6 - 10

*Seeds are slow to germinate, requiring more than two weeks.

**Seeds need light to germinate. Pat into the soil; do not bury deeply.

• Use a timer to control the number of hours of light the plants receive. Seedlings grown under lights for 16 to 18 hours a day should produce strong transplants.

• Fill small, clean **cell packs** (three, four, or six units grouped together, each containing one plant), or peat pots (with drainage holes), with sterile potting soil, and plant seeds according to packet directions.

• Keep soil evenly moist, watering with a spray bottle filled with lukewarm water.

• When seedlings show three or more leaves, begin regular fertilization. A soluble houseplant fertilizer that contains extra phosphorus, such as 10-45-20 or 5-50-17, is excellent for developing a good root system. Apply according to label directions.

• If seedlings appear to be leaning toward the light, turn them regularly. If seedlings are pale and spindly, they are not getting enough light and will not make good transplants.

Purchased kits make seed starting easy by providing everything you need except air, water, and sunshine.

Young transplants may need protection from a late spring frost.

COLD FRAMES, ROW COVERS, AND CLOCHES

During the winter or early spring, you can start transplants in an outdoor *cold frame,* which serves as a mini-greenhouse. A cold frame is a box with a cover of transparent material that keeps young plants warm and protected while allowing the sun's rays to pass through. Whether the cover is made from an old window, acrylic plastic, or polyethylene, the effect is the same. Heat comes in from the sun and warms the soil and air, and plants remain protected from the cold.

Because the sun is its sole source of heat, the cold frame must be oriented to the south or east. Or you may run electricity to the cold frame and use electric soil-heating cables as supplementary heat. By the same token, the magnifying effect of the cover can cause temperatures to rise quickly, even on cold days, killing young seedlings. Regulate temperatures by opening and closing the cover manually (this requires constant attention) or, better yet, purchase a lever that moves the lid automatically as the temperature changes.

On extremely cold nights, give tiny plants extra protection by covering the frame with a blanket. Remember to water seedlings in a cold frame, since they are sheltered from the rain.

Gardening catalogs offer a variety of *row covers,* which are like blankets to stretch over the row, and other devices that can be placed over transplants so you can set them out ahead of the last frost dates. Many people use them to get a head start on their favorite vegetables. You can also make your own plant covers by cutting the bottom out of a plastic milk jug or soda bottle; place it over your seedlings. Cold frames and *cloches* (small, clear plastic covers) are also used for hardening off young seedlings or allowing them to gradually adapt to cooler temperatures before planting.

A cold frame can give a jump on the spring season or provide cold protection for fall crops that would freeze in winter.

34

Planting and Care

While many time-saving techniques are useful in gardening, there are no shortcuts for proper planting. At planting time, the plan you put down on paper will be carried out. If you planned with care, planting will go quickly and smoothly.

Building Rows, Beds, and Hills

Plant your vegetables in rows, wide rows, raised beds, or hills. You may use all of these methods, depending on the vegetables and the layout in your plan.

To make rows, level the soil with a rake (a bow rake is best) and smooth it to eliminate low spots that collect water. Break up clods of soil and remove any rocks. In heavy soil or low areas, build the row by raking soil into a ridge 4 to 6 inches high. This height allows the sun to warm the soil for spring vegetables more quickly and improves drainage. Use a cord stretched between two stakes at each end of the row to guide you when working the soil. Large vegetables, such as corn, and tall selections of okra are well suited to plant in rows.

Make a wide row by mounding the soil 18 to 24 inches wide. A wide row can be built up about 6 to 8 inches high to improve drainage but rows this high dry out faster and need watering more often than rows that are not raised. Root crops and leafy vegetables are suited to wide rows provided the plants are properly spaced within the wide row.

A raised bed is similar to a raised wide row but is even wider: 42 to 48 inches wide at the base, 30 to 36 inches wide at the top, and 6 to 8 inches high. Level the top for planting. This width allows for a comfortable reach to the middle, and the height does not invite erosion. Low-growing plants such as leafy greens, vining cucumbers, and melons work well in raised beds.

Squash, pumpkins, melons, and cucumbers are often planted in hills, or mounds of soil. The small mound is quickly warmed by the sun, which helps these cold-sensitive seeds germinate more readily. The shape also improves drainage and provides deeper soil for the plant's roots. To make hills, mound the soil in a circle about 6 inches high and 2 feet in diameter. Gather the soil from all directions using a hoe; then level the top for planting seeds.

Proper planting and maintenance of your vegetables are vital to a healthy, attractive garden and high yields.

Making a row into a ridge several inches high allows for the extra depth carrots need to grow long, straight roots.

Even when you plant at the recommended time, a late frost may threaten the cold-sensitive vegetables. Be prepared to cover them, or the plants may be injured or killed. Cold-protection devices can be as simple as a plastic milk jug with the bottom removed; even a plastic nursery pot, cardboard box, or a tent made from newspapers will do. Or you can purchase cloches or covers called hot caps. Remember that if the temperature dips below freezing at night and the following day is mild and sunny, you must provide ventilation in the plant protectors or uncover the plants. Otherwise, they will be killed by the heat.

Also, when you set out young transplants in the intense summer sun, you must give them time to adjust. Use a slatted wooden frame, lattice, palmetto leaf, nursery shade cloth, or some other shading method that allows only filtered light to reach the plants in the first week or two after transplanting.

Planting

Sow seeds at the spacing given on the seed package. After sowing, cover seeds to the suggested depth or rake from the sides of the row to cover them with soil. Be careful not to cover seeds more deeply than the package recommends, or they may not sprout. Lettuce seeds and other seeds that need light to germinate should not be covered but should be patted into the soil with your hand or the back of your hoe.

Thin seedlings to give the plants space to grow.

Keep the seedbed watered after planting; seeds need moisture at all times to germinate and to establish roots. Avoid applying a strong stream that will wash up the seeds. Watering with a mister nozzle on your hose is ideal.

Thin seedlings soon after they sprout. Crowding will stunt their growth and make them spindly. You can thin by pulling the plants up; if this disturbs the roots of adjacent plants, snip off the remaining extra plants at the soil line with nail scissors. Watering before you thin makes pulling up the plants easier.

If you grow your own transplants indoors or in a greenhouse, you will need to get them accustomed to the outdoors. ***Hardening off,*** as this is called, reduces the shock caused by a sudden change in growing conditions. A week to 10 days before planting time, place the plants in a shaded cold frame or move them outdoors to a shaded location for one to two hours each day. Young plants will wilt slightly in the heat of the day no matter how well they are watered.

Shade frames protect young seedlings from heat.

Keep as much of the soil as possible around the roots of transplants to lessen transplant shock.

Keep purchased transplants watered and out of direct sunlight until planting time. Before planting, water transplants thoroughly. Remove them from their plastic or clay containers as gently as possible to avoid disturbing the roots; keep as much of the soil as you can around the roots to lessen transplant shock. Set transplants in soil at the same depth they grew in the container. Firm the soil around the plant with your hands, and label the plant with the selection name and planting date. After transplanting, water the entire row or bed thoroughly.

Care and Maintenance

The regular care of a garden—fertilizing, watering, weeding, mulching, and staking (if needed)—keeps it growing and producing. Such care requires frequent trips to the garden, so you can watch for insects or diseases while you enjoy checking on the progress of your plants.

Fertilizing

The fertilizer shelves in garden shops offer many options. Choosing a fertilizer seems difficult at first, but if you arm yourself with a knowledge of what your plants require, you can purchase what your garden needs with minimal fuss.

Premium-quality slow-release vegetable fertilizers are long-lasting granular fertilizers that you can work into the soil before planting. Depending on the formula, they should continue to feed plants for two to four months.

You may need to **side-dress** or make a repeat application of granular fertilizer for vegetables such as tomatoes that produce longer than the product lasts in the soil. When side-dressing, spread the fertilizer close enough to plants so that their roots can take it up. Sprinkle the granules as far out as the reach of the outer leaves. In wide rows solidly covered with growth, the most practical method is to sprinkle the fertilizer across the row and let it fall through the plants. Be sure to rinse the fertilizer off the foliage and into the soil after applying.

Water-solubles are fine, powderlike fertilizers that dissolve in water. They are good for supplementing slow-release granular types to boost heavy, long-season producers, such as tomatoes. You can spray soluble fertilizer directly on plant leaves or pour it on the soil. Soluble fertilizers work well as starter solutions for cool-weather

WHAT IS A SLOW-RELEASE FERTILIZER?

Slow-release fertilizer is sometimes called controlled-release fertilizer because it releases small amounts of nutrients at a time. The nutrients of slow-release fertilizer are made available to the soil as moisture or heat cause their coatings (of varying thickness) to wear away gradually over several weeks or months. This type of fertilizer does not have to be applied often, and it will not burn the roots of transplants. Use a slow-release fertilizer that is made for vegetables.

THE FERTILIZER LABEL

By law, all fertilizer packages must state the percentages of the nutrients they contain. The three numbers on the package always represent the percentage of the three most essential elements— nitrogen (N), phosphorus (P), and potassium (K). For example, if the package says 10-5-8, it contains 10 percent nitrogen, 5 percent phosphorus, and 8 percent potassium. Nitrogen stimulates new growth, especially early foliage. It does not bind strongly to the soil, which is why slow-release nitrogen fertilizer sources are important; otherwise, the nitrogen may be washed away before being absorbed by plant roots. Phosphorus encourages root development and flowering and is essential for overall plant health. It tends to build up in the soil, however, and many soils may be too high in phosphorus. Potassium, also called potash on fertilizer labels, is essential to plant metabolism.

crops that must start growing when the soil is still cool, because the nutrients are absorbed through the leaves. In cool weather, choose a product that contains nitrate nitrogen, which is more usable in cool soils than other types of nitrogen.

Because they contain less nitrogen, you may find that organic fertilizers such as bone meal and blood meal need to be applied in larger amounts and more frequently than slow-release chemical fertilizers. Organic fertilizers depend on soil bacteria and decomposition, which is affected by soil temperature, to release their nutrients. Although they are significantly lower in plant nutrients than commercial fertilizers, many organic

Keep granular fertilizer in a plastic storage bin in a cool, dry place.

COMMON ORGANIC FERTILIZERS

Organic Fertilizer	Nitrogen (Percent)	Phosphorus (Percent)	Potassium (Percent)
Blood meal	13 – 15	1.3 – 2	0.7
Bone meal	1 – 4	15 – 22	0.2
Cottonseed meal	6 – 7	2.5 – 3	0.5 – 1.5
Cow manure	0.6 – 2	0.2 – 1.1	0.35
Dry poultry manure	2 – 4	4.5 – 6	1.2 – 2.4
Wood ashes*	0	1 – 2	3 – 10

*Remember that wood ashes are alkaline, so you will need to reduce the amount of lime you add to the soil by one-fourth to one-half.

fertilizers are bulky enough to improve the texture and organic matter content of the soil.

Work organic fertilizers into the soil at least two weeks before planting. To make later applications during the season, broadcast (spread) the fertilizer on top of the soil around the plants like a mulch. If there is room to work, you can scratch it into the soil lightly.

Watering

Regular watering is critical to success. But how much and how often depends on the vegetable, soil type, weather, and temperature. There is no exact formula, but as a general rule the garden should receive 1 inch of water per week, either through rain or irrigation. This one thorough watering is better than several light sprinklings. Shallow watering encourages shallow rooting because roots must remain near the surface where the water is. Deep watering encourages downward root growth, and the deeper soil stays moist longer.

In hot weather, plants need more water. Sandy soil requires watering more often than clay soil. Newly seeded rows or beds need about ½ inch every one or two days until the seeds germinate and the seedlings sink their roots.

The best way to determine when to water is to poke your finger into the soil about 2 inches; the soil should be cool and moist. Also, observe the plants in your garden. Watering is essential at certain times in the development of vegetables, most often when they are flowering, tasseling, or producing pods, roots, or fruit.

Mulching

Mulching vegetables as soon as they are about 6 inches tall saves time and toil later. A 3-inch layer of mulch will conserve moisture by reducing the drying effects of the sun on bare soil. Mulch also discourages weeds and minimizes soil erosion. It will insulate the soil against temperature extremes, keeping it cooler in summer and warmer in winter; root crops stored in the ground are protected from alternate freezing and thawing with a layer of mulch. Mulching will also help keep plants free of soilborne diseases by preventing soil from spattering the leaves and stems during rain or irrigation.

Organic mulches are easy to find and may even be free. They include compost, shredded leaves, shredded bark, pine straw, and straw. One bale of pine straw will mulch about 50 square feet. Inorganic mulches include newspaper, for mulching paths, and black

As vegetable fruit grows, water becomes critical to support this growth.

Chopped leaves make excellent mulch as they cut down on weeds and replenish organic matter in the soil.

As mulch decomposes, it adds organic matter to the vegetable bed.

plastic, which is often used in early spring to mulch the soil around squash and other vegetables that require warm soil. The temperature under the plastic is 5 to 10 degrees warmer than the exposed soil. Remove the plastic or cover it with an organic mulch as the weather warms, and pull it out of the garden when the crop is finished.

Weeding

Weeds rob plants of moisture and nutrients. They also crowd plants, sometimes to the point of choking them out entirely. Some vegetables, when young, cannot compete with weeds. The best way to control weeds is to prevent them, preferably with a 3-inch layer of organic mulch. Mulch blocks sunlight from the soil so weed seeds do not germinate. When weeds do appear, pull them by hand through the mulch.

If there are too many seeds in the soil and the weeds are growing faster than the transplants, you will need to use a small hand cultivator, bow rake, or hoe to uproot them. Do not cultivate deeper than 1 inch or you may disturb plant roots and turn up more weed seeds. You may also use a preemergent herbicide approved for vegetables, but never use it in a bed where you will be starting seeds within 10 to 12 weeks, or the vegetable seeds will not sprout.

Tools and Equipment

Proper tools and equipment make gardening easier and more efficient. Look for quality when you shop; good equipment is an investment that will pay off in the long run.

Keep tools and equipment handy.

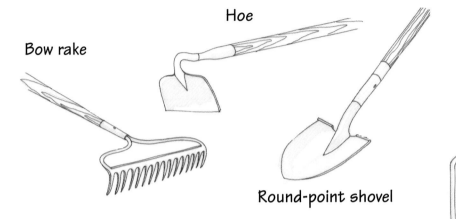

Bow rake

Hoe

Round-point shovel

Spading fork

Trowel

The Five Basic Tools

Although your tool collection can become quite elaborate, five basic tools—bow rake, hoe, round-point shovel, spading fork, and trowel—will do most jobs. Your best bet is to buy brand-name tools. Tool quality and price are based on the gauge of the steel (heaviness and durability) and solid construction (lack of welded parts). Every weld on a tool is a potential breaking point. Wooden or fiberglass handles are also characteristic of high-quality tools; ash or hickory is the best wood for handles.

A bow rake will help you pull out stones, smooth the soil, and work in fertilizer. It is especially useful early in the season for soil preparation. And the flat back can level the surface of planting beds and tap down soil over newly planted seeds.

A hoe is essential for building rows and raised beds. One variation, the Warren hoe, has a small triangular blade and is handy for opening furrows and cultivating in tight spots. The standard hoe has a 48-inch handle; select a length that is comfortable for you.

You will need a round-point shovel for digging holes and moving soil when preparing planting beds. The highest-quality shovels are those with blade, shank, and socket forged from one bar of steel. When buying a shovel, look for a turned step as well. This means that the metal is rolled over on the upper edge of the blade, making a more comfortable place for your foot as you bear down on the shovel to cut through the ground.

A manual substitute for the rotary tiller, a spading fork can be used to loosen and turn soil, mix in manure and lime, turn a compost pile, and harvest root crops. Since this is a prying tool that takes a lot

A spading fork will loosen and turn soil, mix in manure and lime, turn a compost pile, and harvest root crops.

A wheelbarrow or garden cart is indispensable for transporting compost and mulch and makes hauling tools and fertilizer to the garden easier. Try one before buying to be sure it is well balanced.

of stress, especially in gardens with heavy soils, buy one of top quality. The best forks are weldless; that is, the fork and shank are one piece, not two pieces joined and wrapped with metal.

A trowel is a versatile hand tool used for setting out transplants and digging tough weeds. Look for a heavy-gauge steel; cheap trowels bend easily.

Equipment for the Garden

For a garden that is in open view, you will want an attractive compost bin. If the bin is out of sight, however, a simple wire structure may be all you need. You can buy compost bins or make your own from the same type of 4 x 6 wire mesh used to make tomato cages. (See page 45.)

A wheelbarrow is indispensable for transporting compost and mulch and makes hauling tools and fertilizer to the garden an easier task. A well-designed wheelbarrow will support 80 to 85 percent of the load, leaving you to push only 15 to 20 percent of the weight. Look for rigid construction and inflatable tires. Polyethylene wheelbarrows are much lighter weight than steel and serve well for most garden chores. Buy one with a deep bucket and a 4- to 6-cubic-foot capacity.

A garden cart may be better than a wheelbarrow for big jobs such as hauling large loads of pine straw or manure. The flatbed design of some carts is particularly useful for carrying flats of transplants. The cart should be made from durable materials and have rigid construction. Because garden carts have two wheels, they are more stable than a wheelbarrow and are therefore easier to maneuver on rough ground. The cart should be designed to allow easy dumping so the contents will not have to be shoveled out, and the legs should not drag during lifting.

Tillers save time in a large garden, but they can be expensive. Rent before you buy. There are many models available, from small minitillers to large heavy tillers, but all are of two basic types: front tine or rear tine. Front-tine tillers are moved forward by the digging action of the tines. They may be more maneuverable but they require more effort to control. Rear-tine tillers have the engine mounted up front for better balance and handling and have wheels that move the machine forward, so the tines can move faster and break up the soil more efficiently. Rear-tine tillers are the best choice for large gardens and for gardeners who spend a lot of time working the soil.

Irrigation Equipment

Sprinklers are the most common type of irrigation system used. Oscillating sprinklers deliver water in a square or rectangular pattern. Those with timers for automatic shutoff are convenient and make overwatering less likely. Impact or pulsating sprinklers are nozzle types that rotate in a full circle to deliver water to an area up to 5,000 square feet. When set on 4- to 5-foot risers, impact sprinklers provide the best method of irrigating a large garden.

A trickle or *drip irrigation* system is the most efficient watering system you can have. It delivers water directly to the plants one drop at a time at a steady rate and reduces the amount of water used for irrigation by up to 50 percent. A basic trickle system consists of tubing that is laid along the row, a device to control water pressure, a filter to prevent clogging, and a system of small tubes to deliver water to the base of each plant.

A *soaker hose* is made of porous tubing that allows water to seep into the ground. Lay the disconnected soaker hose down the length of a row; cover with mulch. When you are ready to water, attach it to a garden hose that is connected to your spigot.

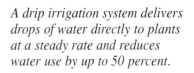

A drip irrigation system delivers drops of water directly to plants at a steady rate and reduces water use by up to 50 percent.

Tomato trellises support vining tomatoes so that they can produce a great deal of fruit in a small space.

Structures

Trellises, stakes, and cages can be simple and temporary or they can be permanent structures in the garden. In any case, these structures should meet certain basic requirements in order to do the jobs for which you intend them. All gardeners have their own methods of trellising or staking vegetables such as tomatoes, beans, cucumbers, and English peas. The suggestions on these pages show some of the materials and methods you can use. Adapt them to your own garden, or come up with your own ways of training vegetables to grow vertically. Remember that the structure must be sturdy so that it does not fall over from the weight of the plants and fruit.

A-frame. The legs of this trellis should be about 8 feet long so that the frame will be tall enough for long vines. A base 2 to 3 feet wide is sufficiently sturdy; a wider base wastes garden space. Build the A-frame from 1 x 2 lumber or strong bamboo poles. Sink the legs 12 inches into the soil and space them 6 feet apart to keep the top crossbar from sagging. For extra support, place crossbars a few inches from the ground and along the middle of the frame. Bolt them together or tie securely with nylon cord. (Jute or cotton twine may stretch or rot.) Guy wires running from the apex of the A to the ground at both ends of the trellis will keep the frame from falling to the side. When tripods are used as the base, guy wires are not necessary.

Tripods. These are three-legged tepees whose design is inherently stable. They are good for containers and fun for kids' gardens.

Quadrupods. These four-legged tepees provide another leg for plants to climb. They work best for beans, as the vines can run up the support and then cascade down when they reach the top. Allow two to three vines to climb each leg. Construct this type of support with pieces of lumber, bamboo poles, or other poles at least 8 feet long.

Small tomato cages are a perfect size for the short Better Bush selection.

Tie the legs together at the top with strong nylon cord, and sink them into the ground 6 inches for added sturdiness.

Stakes. These are essential when growing tomatoes; plants are secured to the stakes as they grow. You can make stakes from 1 x 2 or 2 x 2 lumber, but even pieces of PVC pipe or steel rods work well for low-growing plants, such as peppers. You can buy stakes of wood, bamboo, or plastic-coated metal. For vining tomato selections that grow 6 feet tall or more, use 8-foot stakes.

Always set stakes at planting time or shortly after to avoid disturbing roots later. Place stakes about 3 inches from the plants and use a mallet or heavy hammer to drive them one-fourth their length into the ground.

Cages. Tomato and cucumber plants can also be supported by circular *wire cages.* Tomato branches are held in place by the cage, and cucumbers climb up the wire, making fruit easy to harvest since it hangs in full view. Use a cage that is tall enough to accommodate the vegetable you are growing. You can purchase wire cages or make your own from 6- to 8-foot-long sections of fence wire. Be sure to use 4 x 6 wire mesh or larger so you can reach through the cage to harvest. The cage should be 4 to 6 feet tall and 2 to 2½ feet in diameter to support tall-growing tomato selections. To anchor the cage, wire it to a stake or weave a stake through the mesh and drive the stake into the ground. You can also bury the base of the cage about 6 inches deep.

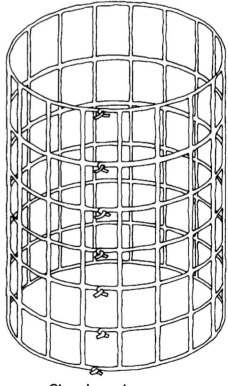

Circular wire cage

Frost Map

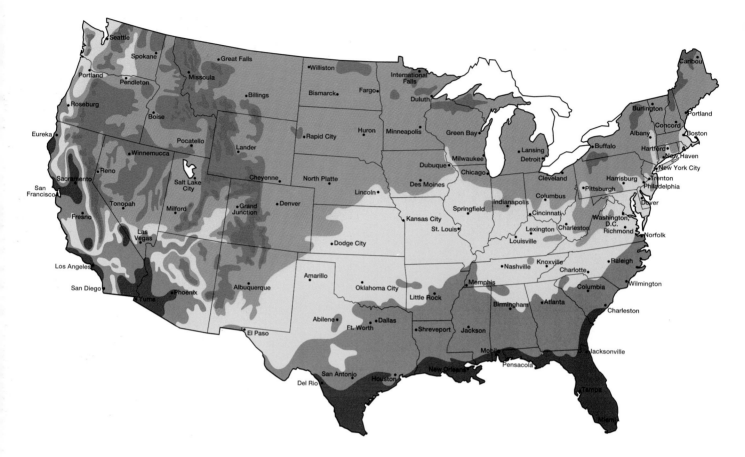

The Frost Map indicates the average date for the last frost in spring. Thirty-two degrees is the temperature normally associated with frost and is the base temperature used for this map. However, it is important to remember that other conditions will affect the right planting time for vegetables in your location. Type of soil, elevation, nearby vegetation and bodies of water, and even seasonal fluctuations can influence when you start your yearly planting.

Key cities are included on the map, but sharp changes occur even within short distances. It is always better to check with your local Extension agent or weather service to obtain the weather data for your area. The timing of the last spring frost is especially important if you want to plant early to get ahead of insect and disease cycles that peak in summer.

LAST FROST IN SPRING
(mean date of last 32°F/0°C in spring)

Before February 28

February 28–March 30

March 30–April 30

April 30–May 30

May 30–June 15

After June 15

Vegetable Profiles

The editors of *Southern Living* magazine selected the vegetables and fruits in this alphabetized encyclopedia based on the plants' adaptability, their value to the garden, and, most importantly, their taste and nutritional value.

Beginning gardeners will find basic information on growing each vegetable, as well as tips to ensure success. More experienced gardeners may want to try their hand at growing some vegetables new to their gardens. The Planting and Care section provides information about soil, maintenance, and plant characteristics. The following are points to keep in mind when gardening:

• Most vegetables need at least six hours of sunlight a day. The exceptions to this rule are lettuce and leafy greens, which can tolerate partial shade.

• The Frost Map will help determine the best planting times in your area, but you may want to check with local weather officials for information specific to your locale.

• Soil tests will help determine your garden's fertilization needs. Work fertilizer into the soil two to three days before planting. Use a premium-quality, slow-release vegetable fertilizer. Apply fertilizers according to the manufacturer's directions.

Other sections in the Profiles suggest when to harvest vegetables, what selections and varieties are available, and how to control common pests and diseases.

For a quick overview of the essential information, refer to the *At a Glance* box accompanying each profile. *Season* refers to the season or seasons during which the plants normally grow and produce harvests. *Warm-weather* vegetables grow in the summer; *cool-weather* vegetables grow in the spring, fall, or winter. Other information includes how far apart to space plants; how large the plant will grow; and how many days to wait until harvest of the full-sized vegetable. Noted also are the soil and water requirements and a list of common pests and diseases.

If you are an experienced gardener, try experimenting with a new vegetable or two. You just may find an unexpected selection that flourishes under your tender care; if not, you can try another vegetable the next season!

A backyard vegetable garden provides many harvests and hours of recreation.

Asparagus

Tender asparagus spears provide a sweet, intense flavor.

Asparagus is a perennial delight for both gardener and gourmet. Within two years of planting, this vegetable will yield succulent, flawless spears. And the bed will continue producing spears, with no replanting necessary, every spring for 10 to 15 years.

Planting and Care

Because it needs a dormant period, asparagus grows best in areas where the ground freezes often. In areas with mild winter temperatures, spears are thinner and less numerous. Asparagus does not grow well in the lower South.

Plant in a sunny, well-drained area of the garden. Without good drainage, asparagus will rot, especially in warm, wet climates. This vegetable likes rich, organic soil with a pH of 6.0 to 6.8; add lime to raise the pH, if necessary. Work a fertilizer into the soil at planting time; fertilize again each year in late winter before growth begins and in spring after harvest.

The easiest way to start asparagus is from dormant **crowns,** the portion of the plant with an underground stem and attached roots. Plant crowns in late winter before they sprout, setting them in trenches about 5 inches deep. Place them 18 to 24 inches apart, spreading their roots, and cover with 1 to 2 inches of soil. As spears grow, fill in around them with a mixture of soil, compost, and sand (for drainage) to just below the growing tips. At the end of the first growing season, the trench should be overfilled to form a 3-inch ridge. This ridge promotes good drainage and helps prevent root and crown rot.

You may also start asparagus from transplants in spring after the last frost; young plants are sensitive to cold. Place the transplants in trenches 5 inches deep. Space them 18 to 24 inches apart, and add the organic soil mix of compost and sand. If growing your own transplants, start seeds indoors in late winter or early spring so that roots are well developed by late spring.

AT A GLANCE
❖
ASPARAGUS

Season: cool weather, perennial

Days to harvest: 1 to 2 years after planting

Plant size: 3 to 5 feet tall, 2 feet wide

Final spacing: plants, 18 to 24 inches

Soil: rich, well drained, pH 6.0 to 6.8

Water: medium

Pests: cercospora blight, asparagus beetles

Remarks: long lived, should not be overwatered

Below left: *Plant asparagus crowns in a trench 5 inches deep.*
Below right: *Spread the roots of the crowns evenly in all directions.*

Water asparagus at planting, but do not overwater or plants will rot. Keep the bed well mulched (about 2 inches deep) and well weeded.

In the fall, asparagus goes dormant after its ferny tops are killed by a hard freeze. Cut back brown foliage and discard it so that the plant does not harbor insects or diseases through the winter. In mild areas where the tops are not killed back, induce dormancy in late November by cutting the foliage down to the ground and not watering until spring. After cutting plants back, cover the bed with 2 to 3 inches of rotted manure or compost for winter.

Asparagus spears emerge in early spring. To harvest, cut them just below the soil line.

Harvest and Storage

Resist harvesting spears the first year; the plants need them to develop the foliage that will produce energy for future crops. You can harvest spears that appear the following spring. (In areas with mild winters, wait two years before harvesting spears to allow for sufficient root growth.) Limit the length of harvest time to four to six weeks the first season; thereafter, you can harvest for up to 10 weeks.

To harvest, cut or snap the spears just below ground level when they are 6 to 7 inches long and less than 1 inch in diameter. Cut before the tip of the spear begins to open. Stop harvesting if emerging spears are thinner than a pencil. Check the beds daily because spears emerge quickly as the weather warms. After the harvest ends, rake the soil to restore the 3-inch ridge.

Once harvested, asparagus spears should be used as soon as possible; stalks toughen with time. You may store cut spears in water in the refrigerator no longer than one week.

Different Selections

The Mary Washington selection has been the backbone of asparagus plantings for years. It should not be harvested until its second year and then only for two weeks. But improved hybrids, such as UC 157, Jersey Giant, and Jersey Knight, are more productive and disease resistant and can be harvested for up to 10 weeks in the second year.

Troubleshooting

Asparagus' foliage may show signs of cercospora blight, a fungus disease that appears in summer. Infected leaves turn brown from the bottom up. See page 124 for more about this disease. Also be ready for asparagus beetles that feed on both young spears and mature foliage. See page 120 for more about these pests.

After the harvest season, asparagus spears grow into tall, fernlike plants that require plenty of space.

Beans

Bush beans produce clusters of beans low to the ground.

AT A GLANCE
❖
BEANS

Season: warm weather

Days to harvest: 50 to 90

Plant size: *bush,* 2 feet; *pole,* 5 to 10 feet

Final spacing: *bush:* plants, 3 to 4 inches; rows, 3 feet; *pole:* plants, 4 to 6 inches; rows, 4 feet

Soil: rich, well drained, pH 5.5 to 6.8

Water: medium

Pests: Mexican bean beetles, mildews, rust, bean mosaic virus

Remarks: plant early, water well, harvest early

Beans are among the easiest vegetables to grow. They germinate quickly, need little maintenance, and yield an abundant harvest, making them ideal for beginning gardeners.

The two most popular types of beans are snap beans and shell beans. Snap beans are harvested for their pods while the beans inside are immature. They are called snap beans because their fresh, tender pods are easily snapped in two; they are also known as green, French, or string beans, though most improved selections do not develop strings unless they are overmature. Shell beans, on the other hand, are grown not for their pods but for the beans inside, which are harvested when full size but not yet dry. Shell types include the popular lima, pinto, and horticultural or ornamental beans.

Planting and Care

Beans have two basic growth habits: bush and pole. Bush beans have a compact, branched form and grow close to the ground; pole beans are vining plants that need to climb a trellis or other support. The two types require slightly different care at planting time to ensure their best growth.

Start all beans from seed in the garden, as they do not transplant easily. Begin planting snap beans and most shell beans just after the last frost, but do not plant limas until two weeks later; they need warm soil.

Beans grow best in soil with a pH between 6.0 and 6.8, but they can tolerate a pH as low as 5.5. They must have well-drained soil or the plants will rot. Fertilize soil before planting, but do not use additional fertilizer. Too much fertilizer delays maturity, causing excessive leaf growth and poor production.

Water beans 1 inch per week when there is no rain. A soaker hose works better than a sprinkler, whose strong spray can knock blossoms from the plants. To conserve water, plant beans in double rows and place a soaker hose between them. Drought-stressed plants may drop blossoms or pods or may produce partially filled pods with shriveled tips. Overwatered, soggy soil can also cause plants to drop blossoms and pods.

Bush Beans

Bush beans grow to 2 feet tall and do not need support. They mature about two weeks sooner than pole beans but do not produce as much or as long, usually giving two to three good harvests over a four-week period. Bush beans require less work up front than pole beans, but they demand more effort at the harvest stage because you must bend over to pick them. Bush beans can, however, be grown in large containers rather than in the ground.

Plant bush beans ½ to 1 inch deep and 3 to 4 inches apart in rows that are 3 feet apart. Or plant them in 3-foot-wide beds, leaving 6 inches to 2 feet between the beds. Stagger plantings of bush beans at two-week intervals through midsummer if you want continuous harvests into fall.

Pole beans need a tall trellis for climbing.

Pole Beans

Pole beans, also called vining beans, are twining vines that grow from 5 to 10 feet long; they must climb on a trellis or other support. Pole beans continue to grow and produce new pods all summer, provided you keep the beans harvested. Two plantings about four weeks apart in spring should supply you with beans until temperatures dip below 50 degrees in fall. Because they grow upward on a support, pole beans require less garden space than bush beans.

To plant pole beans, sow seeds along a sturdy trellis or other support. (See page 44 for more information on trellising.) Allow 4 feet between trellises. Plant seeds ½ to 1 inch deep and 4 to 6 inches apart.

Trellis pole beans when they are 5 to 6 inches high and begin to develop long, running stems. Pull weeds before trellising; then mulch to prevent further weed growth.

Harvest and Storage

Pick beans regularly so that the plants will continue to produce for as long as possible. Harvest bush snap beans when pods are 3 to 6 inches long and pole snap beans when they are 4 to 6 inches long, unless the seed packet specifies otherwise. Pods should be bright green, smooth, and crisp; they should snap with a pop. The seeds inside should still be small. If you leave the pods on the plants until they are lumpy, they will be tough and stringy. At this stage you can shell and cook them as shell beans.

Shell beans such as lima, kidney, and pinto are ready to harvest as soon as the seeds are fully formed within the pods. For the most tender limas, pick while beans are small. Mature limas are more meaty and have thicker skin. Scarlet Runner beans may be used as you would use snap beans, if you pick them while they are young and tender. Horticultural beans (pretty, colorful beans typically grown for shelling) are ready when the seeds bulge in the pods; use them as you would lima beans.

Snap beans will keep for two to three weeks in the refrigerator. Remove limas and other shell beans from their pods before refrigerating; they will keep one week. Or dry beans for long-term storage, putting the dried beans in airtight containers.

Different Selections

Recommended selections of bush snap beans include Contender, which performs well in hot weather; Derby, an All-America Selections winner; and Blue Lake 274, popular for its disease resistance and excellent flavor. White Half Runner withstands heat and drought; Roma II bears pods early in the season. Topcrop produces

Young, thin beans are the most tender.

pods that are fiberless and stringless; Kentucky Wonder 125 is the bush version of Kentucky Wonder pole bean. For bush-type baby snap beans, try Mini Beans and Mon Petit Chéri.

Good pole beans include Kentucky Blue, an All-America Selections winner that is disease resistant. Blue Lake FM-1 produces pods early in the season. Yard Long bears extra-long pods; Rattlesnake is known for its performance in sandy soils. Kentucky Wonder R.R. resists rust; McCaslan will beat the heat (though it must be harvested early for best flavor). Another popular snap bean is Scarlet Runner, an heirloom planted along fences to show off its brilliant red blooms; the pods are flavorful if eaten while young and tender.

For shell beans, try Jacob's Cattle Heirloom, Midnight Black Turtle, and Doss Red Speckled Fall, all bush beans. Ohio Pole is a good heirloom pole selection. Lima beans are among the most popular shell beans. Because of their tropical origins (they are native to Central and South America), lima beans are well suited to hot, humid summer conditions. Recommended lima beans include bush types such as Fordhook 242, Thorogreen, and Jackson Wonder Butterbean. Try pole types such as the heirloom King of the Garden and the drought-tolerant Willow-Leaf White. Good choices for baby limas are Sieva Climbing Baby, Henderson's Bush Lima, and Dixie Butterpea White.

Troubleshooting

Beans are rugged and forgiving. Bush snap beans, however, can be affected by very hot weather; they drop blooms and do not set fruit. Some beans are susceptible to downy mildew and powdery mildew. Rust, a disease caused by a parasitic fungus, is also a problem, as is the bean mosaic virus. Choose disease-resistant selections such as Contender, which resists powdery mildew and bean mosaic virus, or the rust-resistant Kentucky Wonder R.R.

Coppery-brown Mexican bean beetles may also attack and strip the leaves of snap and shell beans. See page 120 for more about these pests.

The pods of immature limas are flat, filling out as the beans become fully formed.

Beets

Beets offer a surprising variety of sizes and shapes.

Beets are grown mainly for the sweet, spicy flavor of their roots. In addition, these cool-weather vegetables produce large quantities in a limited space and are relatively pest-free. Not all beets are round, red roots that "bleed" when sliced; you will also find baby beets (small roots popular for serving whole), cylindrical beets that can be sliced for pickling, and versatile golden or white beets that do not bleed. Many selections are grown for their tender greens, which are rich in vitamin A and delicious steamed or mixed in salads.

Planting and Care

Beets need the cool weather of early spring or fall to develop good texture and flavor. Those grown in hot weather become tough and woody. In spring, sow seeds two to four weeks before the last frost; make three successive sowings two to three weeks apart for a steady supply of roots and greens until early summer. For fall and winter crops, plant seeds in late summer and make three sowings about two weeks apart.

The soil pH should be 6.0 to 6.8 for beets. Before planting, till the soil to a depth of 6 inches, loosen it, and remove any rocks that may disfigure beets. Fertilize before planting, but do not use manure or other high-nitrogen fertilizer.

Soak beet seeds overnight to speed germination. Scatter seeds over a 15-inch-wide bed or sow them 2 to 4 inches apart in single rows 12 inches apart. Cover with ½ to 1 inch of soil. Water seeds gently and thoroughly for good germination.

Each beet seed is actually a cluster of tiny seeds that will produce four to six seedlings. When the clusters are about 1 inch tall, thin to one plant every 2 to 4 inches. Overcrowding will result in small, tough, stringy roots. Rather than pulling plants up, pinch them off near ground level; they will not grow back.

AT A GLANCE
❖
BEETS

Season: cool weather

Days to harvest: 55 to 80

Plant size: 8 to 20 inches tall, 8 to 10 inches wide

Final spacing: plants, 2 to 4 inches; rows, 12 inches

Soil: rich, well drained, pH 6.0 to 6.8

Water: high

Pests: leaf miners

Remarks: soak seeds overnight, prepare soil well

To produce tender roots, beets must grow quickly and without interruption, so feeding and watering are important. Water regularly to prevent the roots from drying out. Mulch well to retain moisture and keep down weeds, which compete with the plants for nutrients.

Harvest and Storage

Harvest beet greens by snapping off the outer leaves when they are 6 inches long; leave the inner leaves to grow. If you want greens regularly, plant additional beets for this purpose alone, as continual harvesting of greens keeps the roots from forming properly.

Pull roots when they are 1 to 3 inches in diameter; larger beets are sweeter but tougher. Harvest baby beets as soon as they are about 1 inch in diameter. Beets that mature in the fall may be stored in the ground through the winter.

If your soil is subject to regular hard freezes, spread a 4- to 6-inch layer of mulch or hay over the row before frost to protect the beets. Or you may prefer to harvest before the first hard freeze.

To store beets, trim tops to within 2 to 3 inches of the root and refrigerate. Beets will keep two or three months. To prepare beets for cooking, leave ½ inch of leaf on the roots to help preserve their color. Boil, steam, or bake beets in their skins, which will slide off easily after the beets are cooked.

Beets produce flavorful greens that make a nice addition to salads.

Different Selections

Recommended selections of beets include fast maturers such as Early Wonder, Crosbys Egyptian, and Red Ace, all especially good for spring planting. Beets that mature 5 to 20 days later include Detroit Dark Red and Sangría. For an heirloom beet, try Chioggia with its unusual white and pink flesh. For baby beets, look for Action or Little Ball. You can also produce baby beets by simply harvesting large types before they reach full size.

For beets that do not bleed, try Burpee's Golden or Albina Vereduna, which has a yellow flesh. (Seeds of golden beets germinate poorly, so be sure to sow more than you need.) Formanova and Cylindra have unusual carrot-shaped roots. For growing beets in containers, try Little Ball.

Troubleshooting

Beets are rather resilient, but watch plants closely for leaf miners. See page 123 for more about these pests.

Although they appear red on the outside, golden beets have a bright yellow flesh.

Broccoli

Broccoli produces a single central head and small side shoots where leaves join the stem.

Vitamin-rich broccoli may be planted twice a year, in spring and in fall. This vegetable-tray favorite needs a long period of mild weather to produce large 8-inch heads like those found in the super-market. In most areas, modest but tasty 4-inch heads can be harvested less than two months after setting out transplants. Continue picking smaller sprouts from side shoots for several weeks to extend the harvest.

Planting and Care

Always start broccoli from transplants. In spring, plant four weeks before the last frost. Broccoli does not do well in the warm temperatures of late spring. For a fall crop, plant in late summer or early fall. The first hard freeze will kill broccoli.

Broccoli likes loose, organic soil with a pH between 6.0 and 6.8. Before setting out transplants, fork or till the soil and work in a 3-inch layer of rotted compost, manure, or sphagnum peat moss. Work plenty of fertilizer into the soil as well.

Set plants 18 to 24 inches apart in rows 2 to 3 feet apart. Space properly, as crowded plants produce smaller heads. Fertilize the trans-plants with a starter solution of all-purpose, water-soluble fertilizer.

Water regularly; keeping the soil moist will promote steady, rapid growth so that the plant can develop a large head.

Give broccoli enough room to spread its few large leaves and develop a large head.

AT A GLANCE
❖
BROCCOLI

Season: cool weather

Days to harvest: 60 to 85 after transplanting

Plant size: 12 inches tall, equally wide

Final spacing: plants, 18 to 24 inches; rows, 2 to 3 feet

Soil: rich, well drained, pH 6.0 to 6.8

Water: high

Pests: cabbage loopers, imported cabbageworms

Remarks: can be grown in spring or fall

Harvest and Storage

The time to harvest broccoli is when the hundreds of *florets,* the tiny flower buds that form the head, are still green and tightly closed. Cut the stem 5 to 6 inches below the head. You can harvest anytime after the head forms, but when the florets begin to open, exposing yellow petals, broccoli is overmature. Its flavor and texture will be inferior to broccoli that is harvested earlier.

In addition to the large central head, broccoli forms small flower clusters or side shoots that are about 1 inch in diameter and originate along the stem. These shoots are usually ready to harvest two to three weeks after you remove the central head. However, if the weather is too warm in late spring, the side shoots will flower quickly. In fall, the harvest of side shoots is more dependable, but be sure to harvest before a severe frost. While you wait for the side shoots to develop, plant another vegetable between the broccoli plants, such as bush beans in summer or spinach in fall.

Do not wash the florets until you are ready to eat them. Broccoli keeps up to one week in the refrigerator.

Harvest broccoli by cutting the central head from the plant just below the point where it begins to branch.

Different Selections

For spring planting, choose early-maturing selections so that the heads will form before the weather gets hot. Try Bonanza, Green Comet, Early Emerald, Emperor, Premium Crop, Packman, or Green Goliath; these are also good for fall. Later-maturing selections, such as Green Valiant and Waltham 29, are best for growing in fall or in frost-free regions of Texas and Florida. Green Sprouting, Green Goliath, and Waltham 29 are also noted for their production of side shoots; Green Comet, Premium Crop, and Green Duke Hybrid have been bred to produce one large head, but they may also develop a few side shoots.

Troubleshooting

Be prepared to protect broccoli from cabbage loopers and imported cabbageworms. Cabbage loopers are green larvae; cabbageworms are green caterpillars. See page 121 for more about these pests.

Although wiry when young, broccoli plants eventually produce a thick, trunklike central stem.

Cabbage and Chinese Cabbage

The waxy coating of red cabbage sometimes gives the leaves a blue cast.

Although they do not look alike, cabbage and Chinese cabbage are relatives with two things in common: they are tasty and are easy to grow. Chinese cabbage will surprise you with its rapid growth, and heads of traditional-type cabbage will please you with the way they withstand cold temperatures in the fall.

Cabbage

Cabbage grown in a home garden offers more variety than those for sale in the produce department. As a group, cabbage include a wide range of crisp, peppery plants that can be red, purple, green, or white; they may be flat, round, or pointed with smooth or crinkly leaves. Cabbage may be grown in both spring and fall.

Planting and Care

Cabbage must mature in cool weather to produce firm, sweet heads. Although this vegetable can be started from seed, you will have better luck and will harvest sooner if you start with transplants. In spring, set out transplants four to six weeks before the last frost. For a fall crop, set out transplants four to six weeks before the first frost.

To grow small, decorative heads (2 to 4 pounds, 4½ to 6 inches in diameter), set transplants 12 inches apart. For larger heads, allow 15 to 18 inches between plants. Some late-season selections, such as Early Flat Dutch or Premium Late Flat Dutch, will produce heads that are 11 inches in diameter if plants are spaced 24 inches apart. Allow about 2½ feet between rows.

Cabbage grows best in loose, rich, well-drained soil with a pH of 6.0 to 6.8. Fertilize the soil before planting, and boost transplants with a starter solution of water-soluble fertilizer when you set them out. Once plants begin to form loose heads, do not fertilize; too much nitrogen can cause loose heads to split. Cabbage heads will also split if they receive too much water, especially if the soil was previously allowed to dry out. Water 1 inch per week when there is no rain; mulch after planting to help keep the soil evenly moist.

Harvest and Storage

You may harvest cabbage heads once they are firm and solid, before they reach full size. Or you may let them grow to full size, but you must harvest before heads begin to split.

AT A GLANCE
❖
CABBAGE

Season: cool weather

Days to harvest: 70 to 105 after transplanting

Plant size: 12 to 18 inches tall, 2 feet wide

Final spacing: plants, 12 to 24 inches; rows, 2½ feet

Soil: rich, well drained, pH 6.0 to 6.8

Water: medium to high

Pests: cabbage loopers, imported cabbageworms, slugs, black rot, downy mildew

Remarks: one of the first plants to set out in spring

If you leave the bottom leaves in place when you harvest the head, the plant may produce several tiny, loose heads for harvest later. When the first fall frost is predicted, harvest young heads to avoid cold damage. Mature heads are more cold tolerant and can remain in place until you are ready to use them, provided temperatures stay above 20 degrees.

To store cabbage, remove outer leaves; wash the head, pat dry, and refrigerate. It will keep two to three months.

Different Selections

Choose selections with staggered maturity dates to spread harvests over a longer period. Early-maturing and midseason selections, such as Salarite, Golden Acre, Early Jersey Wakefield, Heads Up, and Tropic Giant, are good for both spring and fall. Red Acre, Ruby Ball, and Lasso will produce reddish heads. Late-maturing selections, such as Early Flat Dutch and Premium Late Flat Dutch, are best for the fall because cabbage needs cool weather to mature. Savoy selections, such as King and the award-winning Ace, have heavily crinkled leaves. For containers, try Minicole, a small head cabbage.

The size of cabbage heads is determined in part by the spacing of the plants.

Troubleshooting

You may have trouble with cabbage loopers, imported cabbageworms, and slugs. See pages 121 and 123 for more about these pests. You may also have trouble with black rot and downy mildew. Black rot will turn leaf edges yellow and darken leaf veins. Use disease-free plants and rotate crops to avoid these problems.

Chinese Cabbage

There are two types of Chinese cabbage: heading and nonheading. The heading types, usually called Napa, are either long and slender or egg-shaped. The inner leaves are light green or nearly white and are thin like tissue paper. Napa heads mature in about 60 to 70 days; selections include Blues and Michili. Nonheading types, such as

Nonheading types of Chinese cabbage have white, celery-like stalks.

AT A GLANCE
❖
CHINESE CABBAGE

Season: cool weather
Days to harvest: 45 to 70
Plant size: 12 to 18 inches tall, 2 feet wide
Final spacing: plants, 12 to 15 inches; rows, 2 to 2½ feet
Soil: rich, well drained, pH 6.0 to 6.8
Water: medium to high
Pests: cabbage loopers, imported cabbageworms, slugs, aphids
Remarks: fall crops do best

Mei Quing Choi, have loose, thick leaves on long white stalks and are called bok choi or pak choi. Selections mature in 45 to 60 days.

Planting and Care

Chinese cabbage may be grown in early spring, but most selections do best in the fall when days are short and cool. If you opt for a spring planting, set out homegrown transplants four to six weeks before the last frost. Fertilize the soil before planting, and then set out transplants 12 to 15 inches apart in rows 2 to 2½ feet apart. Lengthening days and erratic temperature changes may cause plants to bolt, or flower, so do not be surprised if you must harvest early. If the head develops a central stalk, the plant is trying to flower; you should harvest immediately.

In the fall, you can start Chinese cabbage from seed directly in the garden 8 to 12 weeks before the first frost; sow seeds ½ inch deep, and thin to 12 to 15 inches, depending on the selection. If the soil is too warm for seeds to germinate, grow your own transplants indoors. Fertilize transplants or seedlings with a starter solution of water-soluble fertilizer. Keep the soil evenly moist, but avoid overwatering or heading types will split.

Harvest and Storage

Heading-type Chinese cabbage is ready for harvest when the heads are 10 to 12 inches tall; cut the plant at the base. Harvest nonheading types when the plants are 10 to 14 inches tall. A fall crop will tolerate light frost.

Pick Chinese cabbage early and keep plants thinned; complete the harvest before a hard freeze. Store Chinese cabbage in the refrigerator; it will keep for three or four weeks.

Different Selections

Recommended selections of heading-type Chinese cabbage include Two Seasons Hybrid, which matures in about 60 days and is more resistant to spring heat than the popular Michili. Orient Express is a fast-growing, nonheading bok choi type that is also heat resistant and reaches full size in about 40 days.

Troubleshooting

Chinese cabbage is bothered by cabbage loopers, imported cabbageworms, slugs, and aphids. See pages 121–123 for more information.

Carrots

Short round carrots are best for heavy soils, while long-rooted selections thrive in deep, loose soils.

Gardeners who grow carrots prize these cool-weather vegetables for their many flavors, shapes, and sizes. Sweet baby carrots are ideal for container gardening and make excellent snacks. Short round carrots thrive in heavy soils where the ground is too hard to produce long, slender carrots, which need well-tilled, loamy soil.

Planting and Care

Carrots are a good spring crop but are even better for fall; their flavor improves as the weather cools. For spring harvests, sow seeds four weeks before the last frost. Make two or three small, consecutive plantings every 10 days to extend the harvest season. For a fall crop, sow in mid- to late summer, at least six weeks before the first frost so that the roots mature by the first hard freeze.

The secret to success with carrots is loose, deep soil with a pH between 6.0 and 6.8; carrots will find a pH as low as 5.5 tolerable, however. If your soil is heavy clay or is rocky, consider planting in raised beds and choose short or round selections that grow only 3 to 4 inches long. Long-rooted selections often grow crooked or forked in soil that is rocky or heavy.

To prepare the bed, till the soil at least 9 inches deep and work in compost, leaf mold, or other rotted organic material (do not use manure or a high-nitrogen source). If the soil is very rocky, it may be easier to build a raised bed by mounding good soil or sand and organic matter about 12 inches high. You will need to work fertilizer into the soil before planting.

Sow seeds thinly either in rows 18 inches apart or in blocks or wide beds. Because the seeds are so small, you should not attempt to cover them with soil. Instead, pat them gently into the ground or sprinkle a fine ⅛- to ¼-inch layer of sand, peat moss, perlite, or vermiculite over the beds. It is crucial to keep the soil evenly moist during germination, which can take one to three weeks.

Carrot seeds need cool soil to germinate. To help seeds sown in late summer come up more easily, place a board over the row to keep the soil cool. Remove the board as soon as seedlings appear. Or you may sprout the seeds before planting them. (See page 31 for information on presprouting seeds.)

AT A GLANCE
❖
CARROTS

Season: cool weather

Days to harvest: 60 to 75

Plant size: 1 to 2 feet tall, 6 to 8 inches wide

Final spacing: plants, 4 to 6 inches; rows, 18 inches

Soil: rich, deep, loose, pH 5.5 to 6.8

Water: medium

Pests: leaf blight, nematodes

Remarks: fall crops are the sweetest

Plant carrots in double rows, and keep soil evenly moist.

When seedlings are 1 to 2 inches tall, thin immediately to 4 inches apart or their roots will be stunted by competition with other roots. (Snip off the tops of unwanted plants; pulling them will disturb the remaining seedlings.) Thin large selections again three weeks later to 4 to 6 inches apart, depending on the size of the selection.

Keep the soil evenly moist but do not overwater. Overwatering can cause carrots to crack or split, while underwatering makes them tough and hairy. Mulch carrots after the final thinning to prevent weed growth and to conserve moisture. As the roots grow, the tops of the roots emerge from the ground; cover these tops with soil or mulch so that they do not turn green and bitter from exposure to sunlight.

Harvest and Storage

You can harvest carrots from the time the roots first develop until they reach full size. If pulling carrots from the ground is difficult, water the soil or loosen it with a trowel or fork. Once the carrots are pulled, any remaining tops need to be removed immediately because the leaves will draw moisture from the roots. In the fall, you can leave roots in the ground longer than you can in spring, pulling them as needed until the first hard freeze.

Store carrots in the refrigerator; they will keep for two to four months.

Different Selections

For baby carrots, try the fast-growing Minicor, extrasweet Lady Finger, or Babette, which is prized for its rich, sweet flavor. Short round carrots include Thumbelina, a dependable All-America Selections winner; Parmex, originally from Holland; and Planet, whose roots grow to the size of a golf ball.

For longer carrots, consider the very sweet Nantes Scarlet or the early and heat-resistant Kuroda. A+ is known for its taste and texture; Danvers Half Long is an heirloom that performs well in clay soil.

Troubleshooting

Carrots are occasionally bothered by leaf blight and nematodes. Leaf blight (also known as late blight) will cause the leaves to become spotted and turn yellow and brown. It will kill the tops of the roots. See page 123 for more about nematodes.

Cauliflower

Cauliflower can be a challenge to gardeners, for it needs just the right conditions to produce a good crop. It likes mild temperatures and plenty of water; fluctuating temperatures can stress young transplants, and the heads may split if the soil dries out. But with a long, mild spring or fall and a little extra attention, plants will form good-sized heads, giving you a chance to savor the mild, creamy taste of homegrown cauliflower.

Planting and Care

You can plant cauliflower in spring or fall. Ideal growing temperatures are between 75 and 80 degrees during the day and 60 and 65 degrees at night, so it grows better as a fall crop. (In spring, hot weather sometimes comes too quickly for heads to develop properly.) Be sure to start with young, vigorous, disease-free transplants; never start with transplants that have been allowed to dry out or become rootbound.

For a fall crop, set out transplants in late summer, about 10 weeks before the first frost, so that the crop will mature before the first hard freeze. For a spring crop, set out transplants two weeks before the last frost. Do not plant too early in spring; young plants will form **buttons,** or tiny heads, prematurely if exposed to daytime temperatures below 50 degrees for several weeks or temperatures below 40 degrees for a few nights. (Place straw around plants or use a row cover to protect them against frost damage.)

Cauliflower likes rich, loose, well-drained soil with a pH between 6.0 and 6.8; it will not grow in soil that is too acid. Fertilize before planting. Space transplants 18 to 24 inches apart in rows that are 2 to 3 feet apart. Give young cauliflower a boost with a liquid starter solution at planting.

To form a large, white head, cauliflower must grow rapidly and receive adequate water and nutrients. Keep the soil evenly moist; if it dries out between waterings, the heads may split.

Cauliflower heads turn brownish yellow if exposed to sunlight. To keep them white, you will need to **blanch** them, or whiten them by blocking out sunlight. When the young head is 2 inches in diameter, bend the outer leaves up and gather them at the top of the plant so that they form a cloak to shade the head; fasten them together with a clothespin, or tie them loosely with soft twine. Be careful not to secure the leaves too tightly; if moisture becomes trapped in the leaves, the head will rot.

Harvest when the head is snowy white.

AT A GLANCE

CAULIFLOWER

Season: cool weather

Days to harvest: 60 to 70 after transplanting

Plant size: 2 feet tall, 2 feet wide; 4- to 8-inch heads

Final spacing: plants, 18 to 24 inches; rows, 2 to 3 feet

Soil: rich, loose, well drained, pH 6.0 to 6.8

Water: high

Pests: cabbage loopers, imported cabbageworms, black rot, black leg, mildew

Remarks: grows best in fall

Space plants 18 to 24 inches apart to give them room to grow. Protect heads from the sun by securing the leaves with twine.

Crosses between cauliflower and broccoli, called broccoflower or cauli-broc, are tender and sweet.

Harvest and Storage

If the weather is cool, the head should be ready for harvest about two weeks after you begin blanching it. In warmer weather, it will be ready in a few days. Harvest when the head is snowy white and firm, before the buds loosen. Cut the stem at the base of the leaves.

Do not judge maturity by the size of the head. Growing conditions in warmer areas are not ideal, so heads are usually smaller than those found in supermarkets. If the head of a white selection is tinged with yellow or purple, it is becoming over-mature.

To store cauliflower, remove leaves and refrigerate. It will keep two weeks.

Different Selections

For best results, plant early-maturing selections. Recommended are Extra Early Snowball, Snow Crown, Andes, Early White Hybrid, Cashmere, and Stovepipe. Snowball Self-Blanching develops upright leaves that tend to shade the head on their own.

For colorful raw vegetables, try Violet Queen, which has a purple head (that turns green when cooked). Green cauliflower selections such as Cauli-broc Hybrid and Brocoverde are also unusual and attractive. These crosses between cauliflower and broccoli have lime green heads that are more tender than cauliflower and have the sweet flavor of broccoli.

Troubleshooting

Cabbage loopers and imported cabbageworms will feed on cauliflower foliage and heads. Black rot and black leg are two diseases that affect cauliflower. Black rot turns leaf edges yellow and makes the veins darken. Black leg produces light gray and black spots on the leaves; stems may also become completely blackened as the spots run together. Avoid these problems by rotating crops and starting with disease-free plants. Mildew can also be a problem. See pages 121–125 for more information on these pests and diseases.

Collards and Kale

Collard plants form a loose rosette of broad leaves.

Dependable and nutritious, collards and kale are hearty greens that continue to produce long after cold weather kills many other leafy vegetables. In fact, collards and kale taste better when harvested after the first frost. In areas where winter temperatures rarely dip into the teens, you can pick fresh greens throughout the winter; plants will go to seed in spring. Small young leaves of these nonheading cabbage plants bring spicy flavor, color, and vitamins to winter salads and soups.

Collards

Collards are a traditional Southern garden favorite for fall and spring. Because these greens are so cold hardy, most gardeners can enjoy them through late November, or even all winter long in the lower and coastal South.

Planting and Care

Start collards from seed or transplants three to four weeks before the last frost for spring harvests; plant 6 to 10 weeks before the first frost to harvest in fall and winter. Collards need well-drained soil with a pH of 5.5 to 6.8. Work fertilizer into the soil before planting. Set out transplants 14 to 18 inches apart in rows that are 2½ feet apart; thin seedlings to the same spacing.

Fertilize young plants with a starter solution. Spring-planted collards will not bolt when the days grow longer, unlike other members of the cabbage family. However, collards planted in fall will bolt the following spring.

Harvest and Storage

In spring or fall, harvest leaves when they are 6 to 10 inches long and still young; old leaves are tough. Harvest the lower leaves first and work your way up the plant. Collards develop a strong, bitter flavor in hot weather. In cold weather, frozen leaves may be harvested since they thaw quickly for cooking. A frozen plant is brittle, however; to avoid damage, cut the leaves instead of snapping them off.

Collards will keep for several days in the refrigerator.

AT A GLANCE
❖
COLLARDS

Season: cool weather
Days to harvest: 50 to 80
Plant size: 1½ feet to 3 feet
  tall, 1 to 2 feet wide
Final spacing: plants, 14 to 18
  inches; rows, 2½ feet
Soil: well drained, pH 5.5 to 6.8
Water: medium
Pests: cabbage loopers,
  imported cabbageworms,
  downy mildew
Remarks: good fall crop, frost
  enhances flavor

Curly-leafed kale is named for the shape of its leaves.

AT A GLANCE

KALE

Season: cool weather

Days to harvest: 55 to 75

Plant size: 1½ feet to 3 feet tall, 1 to 2 feet wide

Final spacing: plants, 8 inches; rows, 2½ feet

Soil: well drained, pH 5.5 to 6.8

Water: medium

Pests: cabbage loopers, imported cabbageworms, downy mildew

Remarks: plants overwinter in warm areas, frost enhances flavor

Different Selections

Vates, which grows 1½ to 2 feet tall, withstands cold better than other selections and is the best choice for fall and winter harvests. Georgia grows to 3 feet tall; it tolerates heat and is best for spring gardens. Champion is slow to bolt and does well in winter.

Troubleshooting

Collards attract cabbage loopers and imported cabbageworms. They also suffer from downy mildew. See page 121 for more information. Keep plants harvested to allow good airflow.

Kale

Like collards, kale is very cold hardy and will produce in the garden through fall; in the lower and coastal South, it easily lives through winter. The key is growing it to harvest size before the weather gets too cold for new growth.

Planting and Care

Grow kale from seeds or transplants much as you would collards. For spring harvests, plant three to four weeks before the last frost. Plant 6 to 10 weeks before the first frost for fall and winter harvests. Kale does not grow as large as collard plants, so you should space seeds a little closer. Sow seeds ½ inch deep and 3 inches apart in rows that are 2½ feet apart.

When seedlings are 3 inches tall, thin to 8 inches apart and fertilize with a starter solution. Spring-planted kale will produce harvests until late spring, when the plants flower and go to seed. Fall-planted kale will survive temperatures in the midteens if it is mulched, although a period of severe cold may kill the leaves back to the crown. Use cold frames or row covers to protect plants.

Harvest and Storage

You can harvest kale by cutting only the lower leaves while they are young and tender (4 to 8 inches long), letting the terminal tip continue to grow. Or you can cut the whole plant at its base and strip the leaves from the stem.

Kale will keep one to two weeks in the refrigerator.

Different Selections

Recommended selections include Dwarf Blue Curled Vates, Verdura, Winterbor, Squire, and the heirloom selection Red Russian. Ornamental kales such as Nagoya Hybrid Mixed or Peacock Hybrid may be eaten while young and tender, although they are primarily used for garnishing salads and vegetable trays.

Troubleshooting

Kale is bothered by the same pests and diseases that affect collards. Remember to keep plants harvested to permit good airflow.

Ornamental kale can be eaten but it is primarily used for garnishes.

Red Russian kale is known for its broad leaves.

Corn

White corn such as Silver Queen has a firm texture and a sweet flavor that is considered the best by many gardeners.

AT A GLANCE

CORN

Season: warm weather

Days to harvest: 70 to 95

Plant size: 7 to 8 feet tall

Final spacing: plants, 1 foot; rows, 2½ to 3½ feet

Soil: rich, pH 5.5 to 6.8

Water: medium, important when corn is tasseling

Pests: corn earworms, southern corn leaf blight

Remarks: plant in blocks of four or more rows for good pollination

Enjoying corn at its freshest is a race against time because the vegetable's sugars begin to turn to starch the minute the ear is picked. It is said that you should walk to the garden to pick fresh corn but run to the kitchen to prepare it. A tall, fast-growing member of the grass family, corn calls for ample space in midsize to large gardens.

Planting and Care

If you time your planting properly, you can enjoy fresh sweet corn nearly every day of the summer. Plant early-maturing selections just after the last frost; follow with a midseason selection two to four weeks later, and then plant a late-maturing selection in late spring or early summer. Or stagger plantings of the same selection by planting a crop when the first previous planting has three or four leaves per plant.

Corn likes good, rich soil with a pH between 5.5 and 6.8. Before sowing seeds, work fertilizer into soil. To help ensure complete pollination, plant corn in blocks of four or more rows to create a high concentration of pollen. (When corn is planted in a single row, pollen is easily blown away from the plants.) Plant seeds about 6 inches apart in furrows that are 4 to 6 inches deep; cover seeds with 1 inch of soil. As the plants grow, fill in the furrow and mound the soil around the stems to support the plants. Space rows of early-maturing types 2½ feet apart and rows of midseason and late-maturing selections 3 to 3½ feet apart. When plants are 6 inches tall, thin to about 12 inches apart; crowded corn bears fewer, smaller ears. If you prefer these baby ears, plant corn 6 inches apart, and pick the 3-inch ears when the silks begin to emerge.

There are three main types of corn: regular sweet hybrids; supersweet hybrids, which are specially bred to make twice the sugar of regular sweet hybrids and retain their flavor for up to two weeks longer; and sugar-enhanced hybrids, which have more flavor than supersweets and hold their sweetness up to 10 days after harvest. Supersweet selections, such as Breeder's Choice, have weak, shriveled seeds that do not germinate well in cool soil and should not be planted until two weeks after the last frost. These seeds are slow to germinate, need extra water, and are not as vigorous as other selections, so pamper them until they begin to grow. Supersweets should be isolated from other corns or planted at least two weeks earlier or later than other selections so they do not cross-pollinate and make both crops starchy and bland.

Water corn regularly, since plants will not fully recover when stunted by drought. Watering is also important when the corn is *tasseling,* or producing silks from the tip of the ear. You should mulch corn when the plant is 4 to 6 inches tall; mulching takes time, but it is worth the effort, especially if you live in an area that has an arid climate or experiences frequent droughts.

Try to plant corn on the north end of the garden so that it will not shade neighboring crops.

Harvest and Storage

Corn is usually ready for harvest about three weeks after silks first appear; by then, the silks have turned brown and dry. Test the ear for maturity by puncturing a kernel with your thumbnail. If it squirts an opaque liquid that looks like skim milk, the corn is mature.

Regular sweet corn is about 10 percent sugar when picked. Within 24 hours, half of that sugar is converted to starch. Cook the ears or refrigerate them (unshucked) immediately. Hybrid supersweet selections and sugar-enhanced selections will keep up to two weeks in the refrigerator.

Different Selections

Among regular sweet hybrid corns are Silver Queen, Golden Queen, Early Sunglow, Honey and Cream, and Merit. For hybrid super-sweets, try Honey 'N Pearl, Florida Staysweet, Illini Gold, How Sweet It Is, or Early Xtra-Sweet. Other good performers include sugar-enhanced hybrids such as Breeder's Choice and Kandi Korn. For an old-fashioned sweet corn, try Aunt Mary's, Stowell's Evergreen, Hooker's Heirloom, or Texas Honey June.

Troubleshooting

Corn earworms are common pests. Try planting selections such as Golden Queen with tight shucks that keep out earworms. Also watch out for southern corn leaf blight, a fungus that causes tan to red leaf spots between the veins and eventually turns the entire leaf brown. Resistant selections include Florida Staysweet and Silver Queen.

Ears of corn fill out from the base toward the tip.

Cucumbers

If you make several sowings and keep plants watered and mulched, you will harvest crisp cucumbers all summer long.

For crisp texture and delightful flavor, homegrown cucumbers easily surpass the wax-coated versions found in supermarkets. And it does not take many plants to keep you supplied all summer as cucumbers are both attractive and highly productive. Bush types have shorter vines than vining types and are especially suited to pots and small gardens. Baby cucumbers can be harvested in a little over a month to make gourmet pickles.

Planting and Care

Plant cucumber seeds two weeks after the last frost, when the soil and air are warm. Plants produce heavily at first but lose their vigor quickly, so you should sow a second crop in midsummer to extend the harvest through early fall. Cucumbers like loose, rich soil with a pH between 5.5 and 6.8. Before planting, work fertilizer into the soil.

Cucumber selections that produce 4- to 6-foot vines will yield straighter cucumbers, and more of them, if grown on a sturdy trellis or other structure. Sow seeds along the base of the trellis, planting them 1 inch deep and 4 to 6 inches apart. Thin to 8 to 12 inches apart. As the vines begin to lengthen, guide them up the supports. To grow cucumbers without trellising, sow seeds in hills spaced 4 feet apart. (Turn to page 35 for more information on sowing in hills.) Sow four to six seeds per hill and thin to the strongest two or three seedlings.

Sow bush cucumber seeds 6 inches apart in rows or hills spaced 3 feet apart. Thin seedlings to 12 inches apart in rows and to two to three seedlings in hills. Bush cucumbers are good for interplanting among taller plants, such as tomatoes and okra.

To help prevent cucumbers from developing a bitter taste, keep the soil consistently moist. Bitterness is a genetic trait found in many cucumbers but usually does not become noticeable unless plants are subjected to stress from too much or too little water. Mulch the plants well and water every three to five rainless days.

Harvest and Storage

Begin harvesting cucumbers for slicing when they are firm, green, and longer than 3 inches; keep harvesting them daily so that plants will continue to produce. Once a flower is pollinated, the cucumber will reach harvest size in just a few days. Cucumbers cultivated for slicing may grow 12 to 16 inches long, but it is better to harvest them when they are 7 to 10 inches long, before the seeds become large and the skin becomes tough.

If you are making sweet pickles, either harvest cucumbers when they are 4 to 6 inches long or choose a specially developed selection. For dill pickles, pick fruit when it is 6 inches long. Do not leave any fruit on the vine to ripen and turn dull, puffy, and yellow or orange, because the plant will stop producing.

Refrigerate cucumbers; they will keep one to two weeks.

Different Selections

Cucumber selections developed especially for pickling are usually smaller than those produced for slicing. However, slicing types can also be used for pickling if you harvest them at 3 to 4 inches long.

Recommended selections for slicing include Fanfare Hybrid, Sweet Success Hybrid (seedless), and Suyo Long; all of these are also disease resistant. Other good selections are Salad Bush Hybrid, Spacemaster (bush), General Lee, and Burpless. For pickling, try disease-resistant Saladin, Little Leaf, or Edmonson. If you like heirloom selections, consider Armenian and White Wonder. Poinsett 76 is an open-pollinated cucumber, and Lemon is an unusual round, pale yellow selection. For baby cucumbers, harvest the fruit early, when it reaches 3 inches long.

Troubleshooting

Cucumbers are susceptible to many diseases that attack their leaves, including anthracnose and mildew. To avoid these, rotate crops and choose selections with disease resistance, such as Fanfare Hybrid. Cucumbers can fall victim to spider mites and cucumber beetles. A floating row cover will protect young plants from beetles until cucumbers begin flowering and pollination starts; then the cover must be removed. See pages 120–124 for more information.

Cucumbers that produce long vines will yield more and produce straighter fruit if they are trained up a sturdy trellis.

Once the cucumber flower is pollinated, the fruit will need only a few days to reach harvest size.

Eggplant

Thanks to plant breeders all over the world, eggplant comes in many exotic shapes, colors, and sizes.

Buttery, mildly sweet, and exotic, eggplant plays an important role in many international cuisines. The fruit may be black, green, white, or lavender; one small white selection looks like an egg and is the source of the plant's unusual name. Some selections are oval shaped, while others are oblong and pyramidal. Despite these differences, all eggplants are grown the same way.

Planting and Care

Eggplant is sensitive to cold weather; do not plant it until daytime temperatures are in the 70s, which is about two to six weeks after the last frost. Even a light frost can kill it. Once the air and soil are warm, however, plants grow rapidly, and a single planting can produce until fall frost. In Florida and along the Gulf Coast, you can start the plants from seeds; elsewhere, it is best to start from transplants.

Eggplant likes a loose, rich soil with a pH between 6.0 and 6.8 but finds a pH of 5.5 tolerable. Work fertilizer into the soil before planting.

Space transplants 2 to 3 feet apart in rows that are 2 to 3 feet apart. (Oriental and small-fruited white selections are smaller plants and can be spaced 1½ to 2 feet apart.) Plants will need the support of a stake later in summer, when they are heavy with fruit. Put 3- to 4-foot stakes in place at planting time. As the stem grows, tie it to the stake to help keep the fruit off the ground and reduce the possibility of stem breakage.

Eggplant blooms and produces fruit through summer and into fall until night temperatures drop below 60 degrees.

Plants must grow without interruption, or fruit will be small and perhaps bitter. To maintain steady growth, keep the soil evenly watered and well mulched.

AT A GLANCE

❖

EGGPLANT

Season: warm weather

Days to harvest: 55 to 85 after transplanting

Plant size: 12 to 40 inches tall, 2 to 3 feet wide

Final spacing: plants, 1½ to 3 feet; rows, 2 to 3 feet

Soil: loose, rich, pH 5.5 to 6.8

Water: medium

Pests: flea beetles, spider mites, verticillium wilt

Remarks: water and fertilize regularly for steady growth

Harvest and Storage

To avoid the bitterness and seediness that come with overmaturity, harvest eggplants soon after the fruit reach two-thirds of their maximum size, which varies greatly with selections. At time of harvest, the skin of young eggplant is glossy and well colored; purple selections should be almost black, and white selections should be a clean white, not yellow. The fruit should yield to gentle pressure from your thumb.

To harvest, use hand shears to cut the woody stem that connects the fruit to the plant, leaving an inch or so of the stem on the fruit. Handle the fruit carefully to avoid bruising it, and keep plants harvested to encourage continued production. In the fall, growth slows or stops as soon as the weather turns cool. When frost is predicted, harvest all fruit.

Eggplant keeps in the refrigerator about one week.

Different Selections

Many popular selections yield the traditional purplish fruit. Black Beauty has dark purple fruit that is 5 to 6 inches long. Florida Market is a disease-resistant plant that bears large, blackish-purple fruit. The fast-maturing Vittoria Hybrid produces long, cylindrical, deep purple fruit that is good for slicing. Long Purple is an heirloom selection that yields 10-inch-long fruit. Ichiban Hybrid has soft purple fruit and purplish leaves to match. Pingtung Long produces slender, glossy purple fruit even in hot weather.

For different colors, plant Thai Long Green to harvest light green elongated fruit or Louisiana Long Green for banana-shaped light green fruit with creamy green stripes. Ghost Buster and the Italian heirloom Rosa Bianca produce sweet, white fruit. For container gardening, try Bambino Hybrid (also called Bambino Baby Eggplant), which bears almost bite-sized deep purple fruit, or Slim Jim, which produces thumb-sized lavender fruit.

Troubleshooting

Verticillium wilt, a fungus in the soil that affects tomatoes, can also attack eggplant. A strong, healthy plant will often outgrow it, so you may want to start with larger transplants. Tiny, black flea beetles can also be a problem; they gnaw holes in the leaves. Check plants for spider mites as well. See pages 120–125 for more information.

Harvest eggplant while the skin is still glossy. The fruit should yield slightly to gentle pressure.

When eggplant is overmature, its seeds are hard and brown.

Gourmet Salad Greens

Arugula produces long-stemmed leaves that are best when harvested while still young.

Fresh, cool-weather salad greens are more than just lettuce. Gourmet salad greens such as arugula, endive, garden cress, and radicchio bring peppery and pungent flavors along with vivid greens and reds to a salad in spring, fall, and winter. Because of their varied sizes, textures, and flavors, gourmet greens have become as essential to a salad as lettuce itself. In the garden, gourmet greens also have ornamental appeal, creating attractive borders while providing a fresh market within walking distance of the kitchen.

Planting and Care

All gourmet greens can be grown in fall or spring. Some grow fast, and all can be harvested early; repeated sowings of fast-growing greens will keep a fresh harvest on hand. Gourmet greens enjoy rich, well-drained soil and will flourish in raised beds. Add fertilizer to the soil before planting, and water gourmet greens regularly to keep them evenly moist. For fall plantings, you may wish to shade seeds from the heat while they are germinating.

Harvest and Storage

Harvest salad greens while leaves are tender and young. Also, harvest regularly so that the plants keep producing and do not crowd each other or develop a bitter taste. To clean leafy greens, cut off the bottom to separate the leaves and soak them in very cold water for 10 minutes. Drain well, or whisk away water using a salad spinner. Refrigerate in a zip-top plastic bag with a few paper towels to absorb any remaining moisture.

Gourmet greens will keep in the refrigerator up to one week.

Troubleshooting

The fast-growing, succulent leaves of gourmet greens may be bothered by aphids, flea beetles, snails, or slugs. See pages 120–123 for more about these pests. Rabbits and deer also like the tender leaves.

Arugula

Arugula's tender blue-green leaves have a distinctive nutlike, peppery flavor that makes it popular for salads. Arugula takes about 40 days to reach maturity, growing into a 6- to 8-inch rosette of leaves that can eventually stretch 2 to 3 feet tall. It can be planted in the spring four weeks before the last frost or in early fall eight weeks before the first frost. Make successive sowings, every two weeks in spring, for a continuous supply of young, tender leaves. For all its popularity, arugula (also called Rocket and Roquette) resembles a lowly weed. But do not be misled by its appearance. Arugula more than makes up for its looks in its pungent flavor.

Planting and Care

A member of the mustard family, arugula grows best in soil with a pH between 6.0 and 6.8 but finds a pH of 5.5 tolerable. Sow seeds 1 inch apart and ¼ inch deep, in rows that are 1 to 1½ feet apart. Thin plants to about 6 inches apart and begin to pick leaves when they are 2 to 3 inches long. Water regularly to prevent heat stress.

Harvest and Storage

Harvest leaves frequently while they are young, picking from the outside to allow the plant to continue growing. Complete the harvest before a central stem emerges from the plant. Overmature leaves are hot and bitter but can be steamed with other winter greens or used to spice soups. Arugula's flavor is enhanced by frost, but be sure to harvest the crop before a hard freeze.

Arugula will keep for up to one week in the refrigerator in a dry, airtight container, such as a zip-top plastic bag.

Different Selections

Named selections include Sylvetta, which is somewhat heat tolerant, and the popular Rocket.

Endive

Endive sports frilly light green leaves, firm white ribs, and a yellow central core; it has a stronger flavor than lettuce but is the mildest of the gourmet greens profiled here. Escarole is a type of endive, with less crinkled leaves that are darker green and broader; escarole has a snappy, slightly bitter flavor. Endive takes about 90 days to reach maturity and will not tolerate high temperatures or a hard freeze.

Planting and Care

Endive grows best in rich, well-drained soil with a pH of 6.0 to 6.8 but finds a pH of 5.0 tolerable. Sow seeds for a spring crop two to four weeks before the last frost. For a fall crop, set out transplants in summer at least 12 weeks before the first frost. Space plants 18 inches apart in rows 2 feet apart. For the best flavor, endive needs

The frilly leaves of curly endive will add texture as a garnish or in a salad.

AT A GLANCE

ENDIVE

Season: cool weather

Days to harvest: 90

Plant size: 6 inches to 18 inches

Final spacing: plants, 18 inches; rows, 2 feet

Soil: rich, well drained, pH 5.0 to 6.8

Water: medium

Pests: aphids, flea beetles, snails, slugs

Remarks: has a very mild flavor

Because Broadleaf Cress grows very fast and stays low, it is a good crop to interplant among taller plants such as broccoli.

AT A GLANCE

❖

GARDEN CRESS

Season: cool weather

Days to harvest: 10

Plant size: 6 inches to 3 feet

Final spacing: 1 to 2 inches

Soil: rich, well drained, pH 6.0 to 6.8

Water: medium

Pests: aphids, flea beetles, snails, slugs

Remarks: spicy flavor, easy to grow

even moisture and a steady supply of fertilizer. Give transplants a boost with a liquid fertilizer at planting, and for the rest of the season rely on the granular slow-release fertilizer you worked into the ground before planting time.

Because the center of the plant is so full, water may become trapped there and cause the center to rot. To help prevent this, water with a soaker hose laid down alongside the row.

Harvest and Storage

To harvest endive, remove the outer leaves; the inner leaves will continue to grow. Or cut the entire plant at the base when the heads are full and leafy. In spring, as warm weather approaches, the leaves may develop a slightly bitter taste. For a milder flavor, blanch the head before harvest, tying the large outer leaves over the head. After about one week, the head should be ready for harvest. In fall, harvest before a hard frost.

Store endive as you would any gourmet green; it will keep for one week in the refrigerator in a dry, airtight container.

Different Selections

Recommended endive selections include Green Curled, Salad King, and Très Fine. Escarole selections include Catalogna, Nuvol, Sinco, Full Heart Batavian, and Broad-leafed Batavian, an All-America Selections winner introduced in the 1930s.

Garden Cress

Garden cress adds a hot, tangy flavor to sandwiches, soups, salads, and omelets and is easy to grow. Garden cress likes cool, moist weather and can be planted outdoors in early spring or in fall. It is ready for harvesting in only 10 days, so make several successive sowings.

Planting and Care

Cress grows best in rich, well-drained soil with a pH of 6.0 to 6.8. Plant outdoors in spring two weeks after the last frost or in the fall four weeks before the first frost. Sow seeds thinly in the garden or in containers so that seedlings will be 1 to 2 inches apart. Do not bury seeds, but pat them into the soil; they need light to germinate. Neither thinning nor fertilizing is necessary.

Early Treviso is a radicchio with leaves shaped like romaine lettuce.

Harvest and Storage

To harvest cress, simply pull up the tiny plants. About a month after planting, cress will bloom; you can still harvest it, but the stems will not be tender.

Store washed garden cress in a zip-top plastic bag for up to one week in the refrigerator.

Different Selections

Choose Broadleaf Cress for use in salads and on sandwiches; Curly Cress, also known as peppergrass, makes an attractive garnish.

Radicchio

Cold-hardy radicchio, also known as red chicory, has a zesty bite even after it has been colored by the first fall frost. Many people use it as they do radishes; others use radicchio's garnet foliage to line plates or adorn salads. Radicchio takes from 60 to 80 days to mature and is best grown from seed in late summer for harvesting in late fall or early winter.

Planting and Care

Radicchio does well in soil with a pH of 6.0 to 6.8 but finds a pH of 5.0 tolerable. Sow seeds ¼ inch deep in rows 12 inches apart; thin seedlings to 12 inches apart.

Harvest and Storage

Harvest outside leaves when they are young and tender, and allow plants to continue growing. Some gardeners cut radicchio back to 1 inch after the first frost so that it comes back as small, neat heads. You should harvest the entire crop before the first hard freeze.

Radicchio will keep in the refrigerator for a week in a dry, airtight container.

Different Selections

Recommended selections include Rossana, Red Verona, and the compact Giulio.

AT A GLANCE
❖
RADICCHIO

Season: cool weather

Days to harvest: 60 to 80

Plant size: 6 inches to 3 feet

Final spacing: plants, 12 inches; rows, 12 inches

Soil: rich, well drained, pH 5.0 to 6.8

Water: medium

Pests: aphids, flea beetles, snails, slugs

Remarks: attractive as a garnish

Lettuce

Planted in a border with Swiss chard and spring flowers, lettuce brings out the color of surrounding plants.

Lettuce is one of the most space efficient and productive of all vegetables. These fast-growing, shallow-rooted plants find a perfect home in containers or raised beds. In a garden plot, the different colors and textures of lettuce enliven the landscape while offering you better quality and more variety than purchased lettuce.

There are three basic forms of lettuce: leaf, semiheading, and heading. Leaf lettuce and semiheading lettuce are best for warmer areas; they mature faster and are more heat tolerant. Leaf lettuce, which produces thick bunches of leaves, tolerates more shade and slightly warmer temperatures than other types. Semiheading lettuce, such as Bibb, Boston, or butterhead lettuce, forms a loose head of thick leaves with a chewy, spinachlike texture. Cos, often called romaine lettuce, also forms a loose head, but its leaves have a coarse, crispy texture.

Heading types, such as Iceberg lettuce, perform well in cooler zones because they need about three months of cool weather to form full, tight heads. But gardeners in warm climates can harvest the immature, loose heads as leaf lettuce.

Cos, or romaine lettuce, forms a loose head of crisp, coarsely-textured leaves.

Planting and Care

For a spring crop, begin planting lettuce four to six weeks before the last frost. Always start head lettuce from transplants; start leaf and semiheading lettuce from either seeds or transplants. Since leaf and semiheading types mature quickly, you can make three or four successive plantings two weeks apart to extend the harvest.

Begin planting the fall lettuce crop in late summer, and make successive plantings every two weeks into early fall. Set out transplants first since lettuce seeds germinate poorly when the soil is 80 degrees or higher. (See pages 32–33 for information on starting transplants indoors.)

Lettuce grows best in rich, well-drained soil with a pH of 6.0 to 6.8. Work fertilizer into the soil before planting. To maximize space, you may plant lettuce in 3-foot blocks or rows about 18 inches wide; broadcast seeds thinly over the area. Do not bury the seeds; instead, pat them gently into the soil, as some selections need light to germinate. Water regularly to keep the soil consistently moist so that the seeds will sprout.

Set transplants (or thin 1- to 2-inch seedlings) to the following spacing: leaf lettuce, 4 to 8 inches apart; semiheading lettuce, 6 to 8 inches apart; and heading lettuce, 12 to 18 inches apart. Fertilize transplants with a liquid starter solution.

Continue watering lettuce as it grows. Drought-stressed plants may taste bitter. In very hot areas, lettuce benefits from partial afternoon shade.

Harvest and Storage

To harvest leaf lettuce and cos, break off the outer leaves near the base when leaves are at least 3 inches long. New leaves will form from the plant's center. Or let plants grow until they are leafy and full; then pull the whole plant. For semiheading lettuce, harvest the entire rosette, cutting the plant at ground level. Head lettuce may be harvested in the same way when the heads are softball size or larger; be sure to harvest before the weather gets hot, even if the heads are not fully formed. In fall, lettuce survives until the first hard freeze. In spring, harvest lettuce before plants bolt.

After harvesting, soak leaf types in very cold water 10 minutes. Wash all lettuce types, drain, pat thoroughly dry, and refrigerate. They will keep two to three weeks.

Different Selections

Recommended leaf lettuce selections include Salad Bowl, Black Seeded Simpson, Green Ice, Grand Rapids, Slobolt, and Oak Leaf. Try Ruby for dark red leaves. Popular butterhead selections are Buttercrunch, Bibb, Tom Thumb (good for containers), and the red-leafed Sangría and Four Seasons. Of the heading types, choose Great Lakes, Summertime, or Rosy with red leaves. For cos, try Parris Island or Little Gem for green leaves, Majestic Red or Rouge d'Hiver for attractive red foliage. For a cold-hardy lettuce, try Winter Density (a cross between Bibb lettuce and cos).

Troubleshooting

Lettuce is bothered by aphids and slugs. See pages 122–123 for more information about these pests. Downy mildew can also strike. Try to eliminate affected plants, or choose selections that are resistant such as Grand Rapids.

A mixed planting of different selections shows why lettuce is one of the most space-efficient vegetables for the garden.

Red-leafed lettuce and curly parsley offer the beginnings of a beautiful salad.

Melons

Watermelons such as Tiger Baby are well suited to smaller gardens.

Cantaloupe, honeydew, and watermelon need a long summer to develop their sweetest flavors. Their rambling vines also require a lot of space, which is why older melon selections were once limited to large gardens. However, improved bush types with shorter vines and a shorter ripening time make it possible to grow melons in smaller gardens and in containers.

Planting and Care

Plant melons in late spring after the last frost or in early summer when daytime temperatures reach the 80s and the soil is warm; seeds will rot in cold soil. To avoid being inundated with ripening melons, make two or three plantings two weeks apart or plant selections with staggered harvest dates.

Most melons grow best in rich, loose, well-drained soil with a pH between 6.3 and 6.8, but watermelons will tolerate a pH as low as 5.0. Before planting, work fertilizer into the soil.

Plant melons in hills. Space hills 5 to 6 feet apart for vining types, 3 to 4 feet apart for bush types. Sow four to six seeds ½ to 1 inch deep; thin seedlings (by pinching, not pulling) to the healthiest one or two per hill. If you plant seedless selections, remember that these often germinate poorly. Start them indoors and transplant outside when the first true leaves appear.

Keep the soil evenly moist but do not overwater, especially just before harvest, as this dilutes the sugars so that the flavor is less sweet; a hard rain will do the same. If dry, sunny days follow the rain, leave honeydew or watermelon on the vine two or three extra days to reconcentrate the sugars. (This will not work with cantaloupe, which does not reconcentrate.)

Because melons are susceptible to soilborne diseases, it is a good idea to place five or six layers of newspaper under ripening fruits. Or you can mulch with pine straw to keep the fruits out of direct contact with the soil and to keep down weeds.

Harvest and Storage

Ripe cantaloupes will smell sweet at the stem end. Their skin will have a pronounced netting and will have changed from green to tan. A crack between the stem and fruit indicates that you can separate the

---

AT A GLANCE
❖
MELONS

Season: warm weather

Days to harvest: 65 to 110

Plant size: vining types, 6 to 8 feet; bush types, 4 feet

Final spacing: *vining watermelon:* 1 to 2 seedlings per hill; hills, 5 to 6 feet; *cantaloupe, honeydew, bush watermelon:* 1 to 2 seedlings per hill; hills, 3 to 4 feet

Soil: well drained, rich, pH 6.3 to 6.8 (watermelon tolerates pH as low as 5.0)

Water: medium

Pests: leaf diseases, beetles, aphids, cutworms, leaf miners, pickleworms, spider mites, thrips

Remarks: choose disease-resistant selections, do not overwater or overfertilize

two with slight pressure. This is the best time to harvest. Cantaloupe picked prematurely will not mature.

Harvest most honeydew selections when the blossom end is slightly soft or springy and the skin has turned from green to ivory or greenish white.

Watermelons do not continue ripening after they are picked, so if you are unsure whether they are ready, let them stay on the vine for a few more days. The best signs of ripeness are the dulling of the rind's shiny surface and a change from white to creamy yellow of the underside (where the watermelon rests on the ground). Experienced gardeners can also select ripe melons by thumping them with their fingers and listening for a hollow sound. However, not all selections sound the same, so you must be familiar with a particular selection for this method to be reliable.

Cantaloupe keeps one to two weeks in the refrigerator; watermelon keeps two weeks; and honeydew keeps three to four weeks.

Different Selections

Melons rely on healthy foliage to produce the sweetest fruit, so for best results, plant selections that are resistant to foliage diseases.

• **Cantaloupes.** Dependable cantaloupes include Ambrosia Hybrid, which is resistant to powdery mildew and has long been the flavor standard. Dixie Jumbo Hybrid has high yields of extrasweet melons and is tolerant of powdery mildew; Edisto 47 is good for hot, humid areas, resists both powdery mildew and leaf spot, and tolerates downy mildew. Luscious Plus Hybrid bears heavily and resists powdery and downy mildews. Selections that ripen early and resist powdery mildew include Sweet 'N Early and Solid Gold, which also withstands fusarium wilt. Early-ripening selections are good choices for areas where the season is short.

Musketeer, a bush cantaloupe, is ideal for small gardens or containers; it produces tasty fruit that is 6 inches in diameter. Heirloom cantaloupes include Pike, which performs well in clay soils and yields fruit with an excellent flavor, and Old Time Tennessee, prized for sweet flavor and fragrance.

• **Honeydews.** Try Earli-Dew Hybrid, which bears extrasweet, 6-inch round fruit with juicy flesh; the leaves resist fusarium wilt. Honeydew Sweet Delight matures up to 10 days earlier than most honeydews and has creamy white flesh with a high sugar content.

Pulsar is a classic cantaloupe with dark green ribs and skin with deep netting.

Earli-Dew is an early-maturing honeydew prized for its sweetness and fast growth.

81

Regency hybrid watermelon has the familiar dark green watermelon stripes.

• **Watermelons.** Large, oblong watermelons include Crimson Sweet, an All-America Selections winner that resists fusarium wilt and anthracnose and produces large fruit (averaging 25 pounds). Congo is a high-yielding selection resistant to anthracnose; Charleston Gray 133 resists both fusarium wilt and anthracnose.

For smaller gardens, try space-saving bush watermelons such as Sugar Baby, which produces 6- to 10-pound fruit and is adapted to many regions of the country. Minilee bears round, 5- to 10-pound melons and is resistant to fusarium wilt and anthracnose. Mickylee produces 10- to 15-pound fruits and resists fusarium wilt and anthracnose.

Heirloom types include Amish Moon and Stars, a savory melon with a dark green rind and yellow markings that resemble moons and stars. Strawberry is a long, dark green melon prized for its exceptional sweet flavor. Seedless types include Redball Seedless, a small, round melon with only a few white edible seeds, and Honey Red Seedless Hybrid, a light green melon.

Troubleshooting

Sometimes fruit will not set or will be misshapen because the flowers were not well pollinated. Remove deformed melons from the vine to allow other fruit to form correctly. A few melons will shrivel after the plants set fruit because the vine sheds extra fruit that it cannot support. Seed packages of seedless melons will also include seeds of a pollinator plant; be sure to plant these or the vines will not produce. Avoid using any pesticides that are toxic to bees, as bees are essential to pollination.

Melons are susceptible to leaf diseases (anthracnose, downy mildew, powdery mildew, leaf spots, and fusarium wilt), in hot, humid areas. See pages 124–125 for more on these diseases.

Leaf-eating beetles such as cucumber beetles feed on young melon plants and can transmit viruses that ruin the plants. As a preventive measure, you may cover seedlings with a floating row cover until plants bloom. Aphids, cutworms, leaf miners, pickleworms, spider mites, and thrips also feed on melons. See pages 121–123 for more information about these pests.

Mustard Greens

Mustard greens can be both the sweetest and the most peppery greens in the garden. In fall, cool temperatures convert the plant's starch to sugar, making cooked greens pleasantly sweet. Young leaves have a hot flavor, like that of cress, that will spice salads.

Mustard greens reach full size in only four to six weeks but can be harvested earlier. In fact, the first cooked pot of mustard greens is usually made up of the small seedlings pulled when thinning. To conserve nutrients in mustard greens, do not overcook and use only a small amount of water. Often the water clinging to the leaves after the greens are washed provides enough moisture to cook the greens.

Planting and Care

Mustard greens can be planted in early spring—about two to four weeks before the last frost. The plants need cool temperatures to become sweet, however, so leaves grown in spring will not be as sweet as those grown in fall. Hot weather makes the plants turn bitter, bloom, and finally go to seed. For fall harvests, sow in early fall, four to six weeks before the last frost. A light frost sweetens the flavor of the leaves, but a hard freeze will kill them.

Mustard greens grow best in loose, rich soil with a pH from 6.0 to 6.8 but tolerate a pH as low as 5.5. If the soil is poor, add compost or other organic material before planting; you should also work fertilizer into the soil. You may start from transplants, but direct seeding is best. Sow seeds thinly, ½ inch deep, in rows spaced 2 feet apart. In wide beds, broadcast the seeds over the area and rake them into the soil. If you grow mustard greens in wide rows, one way to harvest is to thin the row by pulling up whole plants just as they become large enough to use. Leave seedlings 4 to 8 inches apart. For larger plants, thin or space transplants to 1 foot apart.

Water once or twice daily in late summer to keep the soil evenly moist and prevent the greens from wilting.

Harvest and Storage

To harvest, break off the outer leaves when they are 4 to 5 inches long, leaving the inner leaves to continue growing. Larger, older leaves (up to 10 inches) that have not been hit by light frost will have a strong, bitter flavor when cooked. In fall, be sure to harvest all leaves before a severe freeze.

Greens will keep for 2 to 4 days in the refrigerator if washed, drained, and stored in plastic bags.

Red Giant mustard greens are prized for their watercolor-like leaves.

AT A GLANCE
❖
MUSTARD GREENS

Season: cool weather

Days to harvest: 35 to 45

Plant size: 2 feet tall, 18 inches wide

Final spacing: plants, 4 inches to 1 foot; rows, 2 feet

Soil: rich, loose, pH 5.5 to 6.8

Water: medium

Pests: cabbage loopers, imported cabbageworms, aphids, cucumber beetles

Remarks: grow in fall for sweet, tender greens

Hybrid mustard greens sport big, broad leaves.

Different Selections

Florida Broadleaf has very large leaves. Green Wave is slow to bolt. Southern Giant Curled is a bit difficult to clean because soil lodges in the curly leaves, but these same leaves give it added bulk. Tendergreen matures in 35 days, 10 days earlier than other selections. Old-Fashioned Ragged Edge, like all these selections, is a popular choice for cooking. Red Giant, a beautiful Japanese mustard, is prized for salads but will turn green when cooked.

Troubleshooting

Cabbage loopers, imported cabbageworms, aphids, and cucumber beetles enjoy mustard greens. See pages 120–122 for more information about these pests.

Mustard greens are always sweetest in fall.

Okra

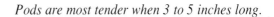

Okra thrives in long, hot summers and produces pod after pod from July until frost, provided you keep picking them. Okra is a relatively tall plant, but bushy dwarf selections grow well in large containers. Its pretty, hibiscus-like flowers form green or burgundy pods that are tender and sweet if picked young. Large, dried pods may be used in arrangements.

Planting and Care

Plant okra no sooner than two weeks after the last frost, when the soil is at least 70 degrees. Okra is easy to grow but the seeds are hard to germinate; before you plant, soak the seeds in warm water up to 24 hours. Okra grows best in rich, organic soil with a pH between 6.0 and 7.0, but it tolerates poor sandy soil and red clay. Before planting, work fertilizer into the soil.

Sow presoaked seeds ½ to 1 inch deep and about 2 inches apart in rows 3 to 4 feet apart. When seedlings are 2 inches tall, thin to 6 to 12 inches apart. Keep the soil moist, but be careful not to overwater because the plants will then produce more foliage than pods. A layer of mulch helps retain moisture and keep down weeds.

Harvest and Storage

Okra pods mature rapidly, sometimes reaching harvesting size just four days after the flowers open. Cut pods from the plants when they are about 3 inches long. If over 5 inches long, the pods of some types become tough and stringy. (If your fingernail will not cut into an okra pod, it is tough.) Use a sharp knife to cut the pods from the stem, leaving a portion of the stem on the pod; pulling them off may damage

Each flower becomes a pod that is ready to harvest three to four days after the bloom opens.

Pods are most tender when 3 to 5 inches long.

AT A GLANCE

❖

OKRA

Season: warm weather

Days to harvest: 40 to 60

Plant size: 4 to 12 feet tall, 2 feet wide

Final spacing: plants, 6 to 12 inches; rows, 3 to 4 feet

Soil: average to rich, well drained, pH 6.0 to 7.0

Water: medium

Pests: root knot nematodes, aphids, powdery mildew

Remarks: avoid planting too early, harvest daily

Burgundy okra pods will turn green when cooked.

the plants. Some selections have leaves that irritate sensitive skin; wear long sleeves while picking pods.

Harvest every day so that the plants will continue to bear fruit; if you leave pods on the plant, it will stop producing. When well fertilized and watered, large selections may grow 8 to 12 feet tall; even dwarf selections can reach 6 feet. But since okra bears new pods toward the top, tall plants are difficult to harvest. You may cut okra back to 4 to 5 feet tall. This encourages branching from the bottom of the plant and may increase production.

Refrigerate harvested pods as soon as they are picked; they will keep up to one week.

Different Selections

For small gardens or containers, choose a dwarf selection such as Blondy, Lee, or Annie Oakley. Cajun Jewel is a dwarf okra that has been a favorite in Louisiana since the 1950s. Semidwarf Burgundy, Clemson Spineless, and Clemson Spineless 80 grow to about 4 feet tall. Spineless selections have pods that lack the classic ridges typical of most okra. Taller selections include Jade, Evertender, and Gold Coast. Cowhorn, a Texas favorite, bears 10-inch pods that look impressive in arrangements. Burgundy is also popular for arrangements; its red pods will grow to 8 inches long.

Troubleshooting

Root knot nematodes, aphids, and powdery mildew may attack okra but frequently do not affect production. See pages 122–124 for more on these problems.

Although short at first, some selections of okra may grow over 10 feet tall. Be sure to give them plenty of room to grow.

Onions

Onions with subtle flavors are usually available only to gardeners, as most of the onions for sale at the supermarket are strongly flavored. If you choose to raise your own, you will discover a world of agreeable onions worth growing in spring or fall, including bunching onions and shallots.

Bulb Onions

Bulb onions are the large, round onions you buy for seasoning and to top a hamburger. They are called bulb onions because they are a true bulb. Most are sensitive to day length, so you must choose selections that are adapted to the length of day of your latitude. Because of this, bulb onions are classified as either long day, short day, or day-length neutral; see descriptions under "Different Selections."

Planting and Care

The easiest way to start bulb onions is from *sets* (tiny bulbs) or from transplants. Choose sets that are firm, well shaped, and ½ to ¾ inch in diameter. Larger ones are likely to bolt instead of forming bulbs. For early-summer harvests, plant sets in spring four weeks before the last frost. (In warm areas, an early-fall planting will produce green onions in late fall; plants not harvested may overwinter and form mature bulbs the following spring.) When planting sets, push them into the ground, pointed ends up, so that the tips are just covered with soil. Space sets 2 to 4 inches apart.

To start from transplants, choose plants that are at least the size of a pencil and that have firm stems and healthy leaves. Set out transplants four weeks before the last spring frost. Onions may be ready for harvest a week or two before those started from sets. In warmer areas, you can also plant in fall for harvests the following spring. Set the base of the transplant 2 inches deep; firm the soil around the plant so that it stands upright. Space plants 3 inches apart in beds or 1 to 2 feet apart in single rows.

Onions can also be grown from seeds sown in spring, two weeks before the last frost, although you will need to wait at least four months to harvest them. Sow seeds ¼ inch deep in rows 12 to 14 inches apart; thin to 3 inches apart. To take better advantage of the wide variety of onions available from seed, start your own transplants indoors eight weeks before transplanting time.

Onions require light, rich, well-drained soil with a pH between 6.0 and 6.8. Fertilize before planting, and keep the soil evenly moist

Red onions offer mild flavors and are good raw in salads and sandwiches.

AT A GLANCE

❖

BULB ONIONS

Season: cool weather

Days to harvest: 30 to 60 from transplants or sets; 120 to 180 from seed

Plant size: 12 inches tall, 8 inches wide

Final spacing: plants, 2 to 4 inches; rows, 1 to 2 feet

Soil: light, rich, well drained, pH 6.0 to 6.8

Water: medium

Pests: thrips, downy mildew

Remarks: bulb onions are day-length sensitive, so use locally recommended selections to prevent heat stress. As bulb onions develop, carefully brush away the soil to expose the top two-thirds of the bulb. This gives the onions more room to expand. Mulch the exposed area to protect it from sunburn and to cut down on weeds.

Harvest and Storage

When bulb onions are mature, the tops begin to turn yellow and fall over. These mature onions have the longest storage life, but if you want a fresh-tasting onion, harvest the onions once they are large enough to suit you. Remove mature onions by digging under them with a fork and lifting them from the ground. Spread them out in a shaded, warm (80 to 85 degrees), well-ventilated place to cure. This helps prevent rot and mold during storage.

After two to three weeks, the skins should be papery and the roots dry and wiry. Mature onions have dry, narrow necks; immature onions have thick necks and are susceptible to rot in spite of curing.

Mature bulb onions may be stored in a cool dry place (45 to 55 degrees) or in the refrigerator. Sprouting indicates that temperatures are too high. Bulb onions will keep three to six months.

Different Selections

Onions are sensitive to day length and will not bulb properly if exposed to too much or too little light. This amount varies for the different selections. For this reason, it is very important to choose selections that are suited to your latitude. Plants will be classified as *short-day* (SD) or *long-day* (LD) onions. Gardeners who live south of 35 degrees latitude, which runs through Amarillo, Texas, and Charlotte, North Carolina, should plant only short-day onions. North of this latitude, you can also grow long-day onions, which need a longer period of light daily to trigger the formation of bulbs. Recommended selections include Granex 33 (SD); Hybrid Yellow Spanish (LD); Hybrid White Bermuda (LD); Torpedo Red Bottle Heirloom (day-length neutral); Excel (SD); Red Creole (SD); Texas Early Grano (SD); White Sweet Sandwich (LD); and Borettana Italian Cipollini (LD).

Troubleshooting

Onion foliage may be attacked by thrips, which are difficult to control because they hide in the tightly packed crown of the onion tops. Downy mildew can also be a problem for onions. See pages 122 and 124 for more information about thrips and downy mildew.

Other Onions

Although bulb onions are the most widely planted, bunching onions and shallots make good additions to a garden.

Bunching Onions

Bunching onions produce a long, white stem (or several stems) but do not form a bulb, which makes them easier to grow. You can treat them as perennials in areas where the ground does not freeze. If you want to grow bunching onions for use as scallions, sow seeds or set out transplants in spring or early summer for fall harvests; transplants or seeds planted in early summer will overwinter and give early-spring harvests. Plants are ready to harvest in 120 days when started from seed, 60 days when started from transplants. Harvest stems as you need them in spring and summer; in the fall, divide and replant clumps for more plants the following spring.

To store bunching onions, wash them, trim the roots and part of the top, pat dry, and refrigerate. They will keep one month.

Selections to try are White Lisbon, White Spear, Evergreen Hardy White, and Evergreen Long White Bunching.

Shallots

Shallots are small, delicately flavored onions that are prized in French cooking. The small bulbs multiply in the ground to produce clusters of new bulblets, but shallots can even be grown in containers. One way to start shallots is to use the shallots sold in the produce section at the supermarket as sets, or order sets from catalogs.

For best results, plant shallots in September or October for harvest the following spring; they can also be planted in March or April for midsummer harvests, but they will be smaller. Shallots grow best in well-drained, sandy loam with a pH between 6.0 and 6.8; they will tolerate a soil pH as low as 5.0. Fertilize the soil before planting. Set the bulblets 1 inch deep and 4 to 6 inches apart in rows 12 inches apart; water regularly, but do not overwater.

Each set produces a cluster of bulbs that pushes up through the soil until the shallots are almost entirely above ground. When the tops die back, harvest the clusters (without dividing), and then cure and store them as you would bulb onions. In spring, divide them and replant the individual sets.

Recommended selections include French Red Shallot and Odetta's White Shallot, which keeps extremely well.

Freshly harvested shallots consist of clusters of bulblets.

AT A GLANCE

❖

SHALLOTS

Season: cool weather

Days to harvest: 90 to 120 from sets

Plant size: 6 to 8 inches tall, 4 inches wide

Final spacing: plants, 4 to 6 inches; rows, 12 inches

Soil: well drained, sandy loam, pH 5.0 to 6.8

Water: medium

Pests: none specific

Remarks: plant in fall for best results

Peas, Green

Snow pea vines are instantly recognized by their colorful blossoms.

AT A GLANCE
❖
GREEN PEAS

Season: cool weather

Days to harvest: 60 to 75

Plant size: ½ to 6 feet tall, 6 to 8 inches wide

Final spacing: tall selections: plants, 1 to 3 inches; dwarf and bush selections: 4- to 6-inch-wide bands 2 to 3 feet apart

Soil: rich, loose, well drained, pH 6.0 to 6.8

Water: medium

Pests: downy mildew, powdery mildew, leaf diseases, spider mites

Remarks: one of the first crops to plant for spring

There are two types of green peas: English peas and edible podded peas. English peas must be removed from the pod, but the entire edible podded pea, as the name implies, is eaten. These cool-weather vegetables take up little space, making them good for small gardens. Like sweet corn, they begin to convert their sugars to starch the moment they are picked, which is why the flavor of homegrown peas is always superior to that of frozen or canned. Both types of green peas require the same garden conditions.

Planting and Care

The key to growing green peas is to plant early in spring, as soon as you can work the soil; this is about six weeks before the last frost. Late-planted green peas begin to bloom when the weather gets hot; they will not set fruit, and any pods that have already formed will develop slowly. Spring frosts will not damage young plants, but a late frost may kill plants that are in bloom.

Peas require rich, loose, well-drained soil with a pH between 6.0 and 6.8. They do not perform well in acid soil. Before planting, work fertilizer into the soil. Water 1 inch per week when there is no rain.

English Peas

Extra-early selections of English peas are very tolerant of cold weather; plant them first, six to eight weeks before the last frost. Plant other selections two weeks later. Sow no deeper than 1 inch. A fall crop is possible in the coastal South if you start in late October; use an early-maturing selection, and mulch and water plants well.

Selections that grow 4 feet or taller require a trellis for support. You can sow seeds 1 to 3 inches apart along both sides of a trellis or about 1 inch apart in a double row on one side of the trellis. Dwarf or bush selections that grow ½ to 3 feet tall do not need to be trellised but will benefit from staking. Broadcast the seeds in a 4- to 6-inch-wide band, leaving 2 to 3 feet between bands. The plants will support each other, but 3-foot sticks placed in the ground among the plants will help hold them erect.

Harvest and Storage

Pick English peas when pods are bright green and almost rounded. Flat, dark green pods are immature, while yellow, hard pods are over-mature. Remove all mature pods so that plants will continue producing. Cook or freeze English peas within hours of picking.

Different Selections

Recommended selections include the dependable Little Marvel, Wando, the mildew-resistant Knight, and Green Arrow. Lincoln, a long-used heirloom, is not as disease resistant as newer selections but is considered one of the most flavorful peas. Selections with wrinkled seeds, such as Little Marvel and Wando, ripen earlier and keep their sugar longer than smooth-seeded peas, such as Alaska. For tiny, petit pois types, try Waverex or Giroy.

Edible Podded Peas

Snow peas or Chinese peas produce the thin, crispy pods that are popular in Chinese dishes. They grow in both spring and fall. As a fall crop, they may be more successful than English peas because the plants tolerate heat better.

Sugar snap peas, flavorful hybrids of English peas and snow peas, have thicker, edible green pods. Sugar snaps have greater disease resistance and hold their sweetness longer than either parent. Grow sugar snaps as you would other green peas. Some gardeners recommend presprouting the seeds to aid germination in early-spring plantings. (See page 31 for information on this technique.)

Harvest and Storage

Harvest the wide, flat pods when they are 1½ to 2½ inches long. Harvest sugar snaps anytime after pods reach 2 inches, but do not let peas become overmature. You may have to remove strings of sugar snaps before cooking.

When unshelled, sugar snaps and snow peas keep for five days in the refrigerator but may lose their sweetness.

Different Selections

Selections of edible podded peas include Oregon Giant, Norli, and Snowbird, a dwarf type that is good for fall. Selections of sugar snap hybrids include the compact and stringless Sugar Daddy, the award-winning Sugar Ann, Sugar Pod II, Sugar Snap, which is good for shelling, and Sugar Bon, an early-maturing dwarf sugar snap.

Troubleshooting

All types of peas can fall victim to downy and powdery mildews, leaf diseases, and spider mites. See pages 122 and 124 for more information on these problems.

Bush-type green peas support each other in a tangled mound.

Sugar Snap, an edible podded pea, needs a trellis to hold up its 6- to 8-foot vines.

Peas, Southern

Southern peas produce thick pods that protect the peas from summer's searing heat.

Forgiving of drought and poor soil, Southern peas are essential parts of classic country cuisine. Black-eyed peas, crowder peas, lady peas, and purple hull peas are examples of these beanlike staples. Southern peas are also referred to as field peas.

Planting and Care

Thriving in long, hot summers, Southern peas do well in poor soil, provided it is well drained. Not surprisingly, Southern peas are sensitive to frost and need warm soil to germinate. Plant them in late spring, two to three weeks after the last frost. For fall crops, sow in mid- to late summer, at least six weeks before the first frost. (To speed germination, soak the seeds overnight before planting them.)

Sow seeds in rows that are 2 feet apart or in 18-inch-wide beds. Plant them 6 inches apart; they should be planted 1 inch deep in clay soil or 2 inches deep in sandy soil. Southern peas grow best in average, well-drained soil with a pH between 6.0 and 6.8 but will tolerate soil with a pH of 5.5. They need little or no fertilizer; do not feed plants any nitrogen because you will get all leaves and no peas. In fact, Southern peas actually produce their own nitrogen in the soil, leaving the ground richer than before they were planted.

Although drought tolerant, Southern peas will yield more if the soil is evenly moist. But avoid overwatering, especially at blooming time, as this can delay the formation of pods. Plants may also stop setting pods if daytime temperatures remain above 95 degrees for a week, but they will begin again when temperatures drop.

Harvest and Storage

Peas are ready for harvest in 60 to 90 days, depending on the selection. The best time for harvesting is indicated by the color of the pod. Purple hull selections are ready when the ends and almost half of the pod have turned from green to purple. If the pod is completely purple, the seeds will be too dry.

Harvest other types when the pods begin to change from green to yellow or tan. The peas should be pale green inside the pod. If left unharvested, peas will become "rattle dry" in a few days and will attract weevils and other insects. Be sure to harvest before they reach this stage so that plants will continue producing. Depending on the selection, you may get four harvests from a single planting.

Shelled or unshelled, Southern peas will keep one week in the refrigerator. Store shelled peas in an airtight container.

Different Selections

Crowder peas are among the most productive. Recommended selections include Mississippi Silver Brown Crowder, Calico, and Colossus. For purple hull peas, try Purple Hull 49, Pinkeye Purple Hull, Mississippi Pinkeye, and Mississippi Purple Hull.

For white or cream types, try Zipper Cream (the pods have a "zipper" for easy shelling), Mississippi Cream, Running Conch, and Texas Cream 40. (Small-seeded cream types are also called lady peas.)

Black-eyed peas perform best in warm, dry weather; try Queen Anne, California No. 5 Black Eye, and Magnolia Blackeye. An heirloom type that resists hot, dry weather is Big Red Ripper.

Troubleshooting

Southern peas do a remarkable job of fighting off insects and diseases but may occasionally have problems. If you have trouble with nematodes, try Bettergreen, Bettergrow, or the Mississippi selections, which have been bred for resistance. The latter are also resistant to fusarium wilt, as are Elite and Early Acre. Mexican bean beetles may feed on the leaves but can be picked off the plants. See pages 120 and 125 for more information about these insects and diseases.

Small peas are best shelled by hand.

Harvest Southern peas before the pods begin to change color. Peas in purple pods may be too dry, but pick them anyway to keep the plant producing.

Peppers

Peppers grow in all shapes and sizes.

Peppers come from all over the world in a variety of shapes and colors. Small, shrublike plants with dainty white flowers and colorful fruits, peppers are as ornamental as they are productive, mixing with flowers and herbs in a garden or in a pot. Despite their variety, all peppers fall into one of two groups: sweet and hot. Both types are grown in the same conditions, and most produce continually from summer to fall.

Planting and Care

The best way to grow peppers is from transplants. Plants take a long time to mature if grown from seed, and seed can be stubborn about germinating. Select only small, healthy transplants with dark green foliage and no flowers to achieve the best results. Transplants that are blooming will not be as productive as those without blooms. To grow your own transplants, start seeds indoors six to eight weeks before planting time. Seeds are finicky, so drop two or three into each pot and thin any extras later. (See page 32 for information on starting seed indoors.)

Peppers are sensitive to cold. Do not set out transplants until nights are above 60 degrees, generally two to four weeks after the last frost. Spacing depends on the size of the mature plant, which varies among selections; most should be spaced 18 to 24 inches apart in rows that are 2 to 3 feet apart. Stake plants to keep them from falling over or breaking under the weight of the fruit.

Peppers require fertile, well-drained soil with a pH between 6.0 and 6.8, although they can tolerate a pH as low as 5.5. Work fertilizer into the soil before planting, and feed with a liquid starter solution after setting out transplants. Do not overfertilize, as this can cause the blossoms to drop.

Keep the soil evenly moist, especially when plants are blooming and setting fruit. Drought also causes dropped blossoms and smaller fruit. Mulch will help prevent the soil from drying out.

AT A GLANCE
❖
PEPPERS

Season: warm weather

Days to harvest: 55 to 75

Plant size: 1 to 3 feet tall, 1 to 2 feet wide

Final spacing: plants, 18 to 24 inches; rows, 2 to 3 feet

Soil: fertile, well drained, pH 5.5 to 6.8

Water: medium

Pests: Tobacco Mosaic Virus, nematodes

Remarks: do not overfertilize, do not plant too early

Harvest and Storage

You can harvest peppers as soon as they reach a usable size or let them continue to grow to their mature size. Cut the short, woody stems on each fruit with shears or a sharp knife rather than pulling or twisting the peppers off the plant. Leave about ½ inch of stem on the fruit. When frost is predicted, pick all peppers and store them in the refrigerator. Use the smaller peppers first; healthy peppers that are nearly full size will keep for several weeks in the refrigerator. Hot peppers that are intended for drying should turn completely red before being harvested. Remember to wear plastic gloves while handling hot peppers, such as Tabasco, Serrano, or Habañero, to avoid burning your skin.

In their native habitat, peppers are perennial. Some gardeners take advantage of this by transplanting their hard-to-come-by selections into containers before the first freeze in fall and placing them near a sunny window indoors to overwinter. Use liquid fertilizer twice a month during the winter until you are ready to set the plants back out in late spring.

Different Selections

There are hundreds of pepper selections available. Some are heirloom or ethnic selections that are locally distributed. Many of the tastiest peppers are difficult to find as commercially grown transplants, so be prepared to grow your own transplants.

• **Sweet Peppers.** Sweet peppers come in many shapes and sizes. The tart green bell pepper that many gardeners grow is typically harvested at the immature green stage, but if left to ripen on the vine, most bell peppers will turn red, purple, orange, or yellow, depending on the selection. These ripe peppers are sweeter, more flavorful, and higher in vitamins A and C. However, if you let peppers mature, the plant will not produce many new fruits. Set out additional plants if you plan to let the peppers fully ripen.

Recommended bell pepper selections include the bright orange Valencia and Corona, the butterscotch yellow Golden Summer TMV, and the striking Purple Beauty. Three good bell peppers that ripen to red are Whopper Improved Hybrid, Keystone Resistant Giant, and Peto Wonder. With the exception of Purple Beauty, these selections resist Tobacco Mosaic Virus.

Other sweet peppers are loosely grouped as salad peppers but can be used for cooking, canning, or drying. They include pimiento,

Bell peppers require frequent watering during dry weather to produce large, well-shaped fruit.

cherry, banana, and cubanelle peppers. Among the heart-shaped pimiento peppers is the popular Gypsy, an All-America Selections winner that ripens to orange red. It is both productive and suitable for container gardening. Perfection, a very flavorful pimiento pepper that ripens to red, is good for drenching in olive oil and roasting.

Cherry peppers are flavorful and are good for canning or pickling.

Cherry peppers are small, rounded, sweet red peppers. Red Cherry is an heirloom that looks like a cherry tomato and has a deep, rich flavor. Banana peppers are named for their long, tapered fruit that changes from light green to yellow. Sweet Banana is a dependable favorite. Light green cubanelle peppers are tapered and thin skinned and have thick, sweet flesh. They are good raw in salads, or stuffed or fried. Biscayne Hybrid's dense foliage protects the thin-skinned peppers from sunscald.

The red heirloom sweet pepper Lemme's Italian Sweet looks like a hot pepper. This pepper dries well, even if grown in humid areas.

Thin-skinned cubanelles are the sweet peppers preferred by European cooks.

• **Hot Peppers.** Hot peppers range from very mild to unbearably hot. For comparison, the pungency of peppers is measured in units called Scoville Heat units. Sweet bell peppers measure zero, and mild Anaheims measure only 1,000 units. Jalapeño and cayenne peppers usually measure between 2,500 and 4,000 units. And at the opposite end of the chart are tabasco peppers, which have a burn of 60,000 to 80,000 Scoville Heat units.

Hungarian Yellow Wax is a long, tapered yellow pepper with a mild flavor; it is popular for salads and for canning. Anaheim Chili is medium hot and is often cooked with other vegetables or used in Southwestern cuisine. Jalapeño and cayenne are good for making pepper vinegar and are often used in Mexican food. Louisiana Hot is a productive Southern heirloom that is popular for hot sauce. Giant Thai Hot is suitable for zesty Thai and Chinese recipes. Super Chili is an All-America Selections winner that is both productive and ornamental. Serrano, which is very hot but flavorful, is a good choice for chili sauce and salsa. Long Red dries well. And for the hottest peppers, try habañero.

Troubleshooting

Most sweet pepper plants are sensitive to fluctuations in temperature. They may drop blossoms when night temperatures are lower than 55 degrees or higher than 75 to 80 degrees or when day temperatures exceed 90 degrees. They will resume setting fruit when temperatures return to normal. (Hot peppers and small sweet peppers, such as cherry types, are more tolerant of high temperatures than larger sweet peppers.) Like tomatoes, peppers occasionally suffer from sunscald, but those with heavy foliage are less likely to be afflicted because the leaves protect the fruit. Partial shade in very hot climates also helps. Stake peppers so that plants do not fall over, thus making fruit more susceptible to disease and insects.

Tobacco Mosaic Virus (or TMV) is a disease that probably will not kill the plant but may reduce yields. To avoid TMV, plant resistant selections. Peppers are also threatened by nematodes. See pages 123 and 125 for more on TMV and nematodes.

Above: *Pick banana peppers when they are light green or yellow; this encourages continued production.*

Cayennes are long, slim hot peppers with pointed ends.

Potatoes

Dig up potatoes in early summer about the same time onions are ready to harvest.

AT A GLANCE
❖
POTATOES

Season: cool weather

Days to harvest: 60 to 90

Plant size: 2 feet tall,
1 foot wide

Final spacing: plants, 12 inches;
furrows, 3 feet

Soil: rich, loose, well drained,
pH 5.0 to 6.8

Water: medium

Pests: leaf blight, aphids,
Colorado potato beetles, flea
beetles, European corn
borers, blister beetles

Remarks: plant only certified
seed potatoes

Potatoes are compact plants that fit into any kitchen garden. They can even be grown in containers or bottomless baskets to yield a crop of tender new potatoes within eight weeks of planting. Potatoes are a good crop for children, too, as each potato dug up is a surprise.

Planting and Care

Potatoes may be grown in spring or in fall. The easiest way to start them is from *seed potatoes,* or certified disease-free potatoes that will be cut into pieces for planting. Store seed potatoes, uncut, in the refrigerator until a week before planting; during the last week store them at room temperature. A day or two before planting, cut large seed potatoes into pieces about the size of small eggs. Each piece should have one or two *eyes* (recessed growth buds). Let pieces remain exposed to air until they look calloused; this exposure will guard against rot.

For a late-spring harvest, plant four to six weeks before the last frost. A late frost may nip young plants back, but they will usually recover. For a fall crop, plant again in mid- to late summer in order to harvest before the first hard freeze, which kills the plants.

Potatoes like rich, loose, well-drained soil that has a pH between 6.0 and 6.8, although they can tolerate a pH as low as 5.0. They will even grow in sandy soil. Before planting, work fertilizer into the soil. Plant the seed pieces 12 inches apart in furrows that are 3 feet apart; set them 3½ inches deep in clay soil and 6 inches deep in sandy soil. Set the pieces so that the eyes face upward.

As the plants grow, mound the soil around the stems to a height of about 8 inches, and then mulch to keep the soil moist. Mounding encourages potatoes to develop and protects them from exposure to light, which turns them green. (Any green areas should be peeled or cut away before the potato is cooked.) In heavy clay soil, you can cover the stems with a compost-and-sand mixture, pine straw, or other organic mulch instead of mounding with soil.

Water plants during dry periods so that the soil stays evenly moist, especially when potatoes begin to form (six to eight weeks after planting), or they will be cracked or misshapen.

Harvest and Storage

New potatoes are the small, immature potatoes prized for their sweetness and tenderness. They are ready for harvest about eight weeks after planting. Dig carefully with your fingers several inches below the ground in an area 12 to 18 inches around the plant. Gently pull and lift the potatoes from the ground. Be careful not to uproot the plants, which the remaining potatoes depend on to reach maturity. Because of their high moisture content, new potatoes should not be stored.

Potatoes are fully mature when the foliage begins to turn yellow and die back, but you should leave them in the ground two to three weeks longer. The tough skin that develops during this period helps protect the potato from damage during harvest and lengthens storage life.

Clean potatoes by wiping the soil off with a soft brush. Or spread them out and spray with a gentle stream of water. Never wash them in a tub of water, as any decay organisms on the potatoes may spread to other potatoes. Place potatoes in a shaded location until completely dry.

To store potatoes, put them in a dark, humid, cool location (between 35 and 50 degrees) or refrigerate them. They will keep two to three months if spread out in a single layer for good air circulation.

Different Selections

Plant only certified seed potatoes that have been grown in carefully controlled, disease-free conditions. Do not use potatoes from the supermarket, as these are often chemically treated to prevent sprouting. Purchase seed potatoes from a local farm supply store or a mail-order source that lists specific selections.

Recommended white-skinned selections include Kennebec, an all-purpose potato with high yields in midseason; it thrives under adverse conditions, is resistant to late-season blight, and produces potatoes with flaky, white flesh. Yukon Gold, an early- to midseason potato, has yellow skin and rich yellow flesh that is good for baking, boiling, or frying. Yellow Finn is a small to medium-sized potato with a deep yellow color and a naturally buttery taste.

Red-skinned selections include Red Pontiac, an early-maturing type that does well in heavy soils and produces new potatoes with excellent flavor. Desiree has high yields of potatoes with creamy flesh and smooth, blush-colored skin. Cherries Jubilee, an heirloom selection, is prized for its delicious flavor.

Troubleshooting

Potatoes are vulnerable to disease, especially leaf blight (watch for dark spots or mold on the underside of leaves). Choose early-maturing and disease-resistant types. Potatoes can also attract aphids, Colorado potato beetles, flea beetles, European corn borers, and blister beetles. See pages 120–122 for information about these pests.

Cut up seed potatoes several days before planting, leaving at least two eyes on each egg-sized piece.

Mound the soil to create extra room for more potatoes to form and to protect them from sunlight.

Potatoes, Sweet

Sweet potatoes will vary in size and shape.

One of the few vegetables that thrive in hot weather, sweet potatoes make their way to the table by late summer or early fall. They are high in vitamins and fiber. Most selections require a lot of space to grow, but some have compact vines that are better suited to small gardens. Sweet potato selections grown in warmer regions are often called yams; they have a moist flesh, unlike the drier selections grown in cool climates.

Planting and Care

Sweet potatoes can be planted anytime from three weeks after the last frost until early summer, as long as they have enough time to mature before the fall frost. Start from young plants, or *slips* (also called draws, poles, or transplants). Buy only certified, disease-free plants from a seed store or mail-order source.

Sweet potatoes like loose soil that is well drained and has a pH between 6.0 and 6.8; they will tolerate a soil pH as low as 5.0. If grown in heavy clay soil, sweet potatoes may be rough and irregular. In poor, infertile soil, work in a low-nitrogen fertilizer such as 5-10-10 before planting. (Too much nitrogen reduces yield and lowers quality.)

Sweet potatoes are grown in mounded rows 10 inches high and 12 inches wide. Leave 3 to 4 feet between rows. Set slips 4 to 5 inches deep and 12 to 15 inches apart and keep the soil moist until the slips are established. Once established, sweet potatoes can withstand more dry weather than many other vegetables. But roots will crack when they take in a lot of water after a long, dry period; a constant supply of moisture will prevent this.

Harvest and Storage

Sweet potatoes should reach maturity 100 to 120 days after planting, but they will keep growing until you harvest them or until frost kills the plants. As the potatoes become larger, they may crack the surface of the ground. Before you harvest, note whether the soil has begun to crack and dig a few potatoes to check their size. If they are fully formed, harvest the crop, digging carefully. Potatoes that are cut or bruised are more likely to rot in storage. Very small potatoes may not store well, so plan to use them first. Be sure to harvest before a frost; it is really best to harvest before temperatures dip below 50 degrees.

Let sweet potatoes dry a few hours on the ground; then cure them to help prevent rot during storage and to improve sweetness and flavor. (Uncured sweet potatoes taste musty and earthy.) To cure,

---

AT A GLANCE

❖

SWEET POTATOES

Season: warm weather

Days to harvest: 100 to 120

Plant size: 1 foot tall, 3 to 6 feet wide

Final spacing: plants, 12 to 15 inches; rows, 3 to 4 feet

Soil: loose, well drained, pH 5.0 to 6.8

Water: low to medium

Pests: sweet potato weevils, beetles

Remarks: use only certified, disease-free plants

spread the potatoes in a dark, well-ventilated place where temperatures are above 70 degrees, such as near a furnace, water heater, or clothes dryer. After about a week, they should be ready for packing in boxes and storing in a cooler, humid location (55 to 60 degrees and 85 percent relative humidity).

Sweet potatoes will keep two to three months under these conditions.

Different Selections

One of the most popular selections is Centennial, a heavy producer of sweet potatoes with smooth skin and deep orange flesh. Beauregard is a high-yielding selection of potatoes with light purple skin, uniform shape, and dark orange flesh. For small gardens, try bush types like Bush Porto Rico; potatoes have copper-colored skin and moist reddish-orange flesh that is excellent for baking. Vardaman is another bush type that yields many potatoes and has attractive deep red and green foliage.

Troubleshooting

Sweet potatoes are affected by potassium deficiencies in the soil, which cause the roots to be long and slender rather than short and thick. Do a soil test and add potassium to the soil as indicated. Turn to page 26 to read more about soil tests.

Sweet potato weevils bore into developing tubers and can ruin a crop. Planting in a different location every year will help, as the weevils overwinter in the ground. Several beetles, such as flea and cucumber, feed on sweet potato foliage. See page 120 for more information about the beetles.

Sweet potato vines will run all over the garden.

Pumpkins

Large pumpkins require a lot of garden space. The green fruit at lower left is a gourd, a relative of pumpkins and squash.

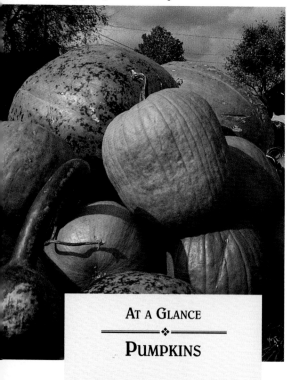

AT A GLANCE
❖
PUMPKINS

Season: warm weather

Days to harvest: 95 to 120

Plant size: vining, 10 feet long; compact, 4 to 6 feet long

Final spacing: vining: hills, 6 to 10 feet; rows, 8 to 12 feet; bush: plants, 4 to 6 feet; rows, 4 to 6 feet

Soil: loose, rich, pH 5.5 to 6.8

Water: high

Pests: beetles, vine borers, mildews, and others

Remarks: grow bush selections in small gardens

Once a staple of the fall and winter diet, pumpkins today are often grown just for the fun of it. If you have a large garden, you can grow a rambling type and win bragging rights with fruit that weigh more than 100 pounds. If your space is limited, you can try compact bush selections that produce future jack-o'-lanterns. For decorative fall arrangements, there are minipumpkins and white pumpkins. If you want to enjoy that old-fashioned seasonal pumpkin pie, try sweet or heirloom types recommended for their golden, fine-textured flesh (some also have edible seeds that are delicious when toasted).

Planting and Care

Plant pumpkins in late spring after the soil is thoroughly warm; this is at least two weeks after the last frost. Pumpkins will be ready for harvest in mid- to late summer. To harvest later in the fall, delay planting until early to midsummer.

Pumpkins are usually grown in hills. They prefer loose, rich soil with a pH between 6.0 and 6.8, although a pH as low as 5.5 is tolerable. Before planting, work fertilizer into each hill. Allow 6 to 10 feet between hills for vining types and 4 to 6 feet for bush types. In each hill, sow five or six seeds 2 to 3 inches apart and ½ to 1 inch deep. When seedlings are 2 inches tall, thin to one or two plants per hill. If you want to grow the largest pumpkin in the neighborhood, leave only one plant per hill. After the fruits begin to grow, remove all but one or two from the vine.

You may also grow pumpkins in rows. Sow seeds of vining types 2 to 3 feet apart in rows 8 to 12 feet apart. For bush types, sow seeds 2 to 3 feet apart in rows 4 to 6 feet apart. In a small garden, small-fruited pumpkins can be trained on a trellis. However, you must support the fruit in a sling so that it does not rip from the vine. You can make a sling with a length of nylon stocking tied to the trellis. Wrap it under the fruit so that it cradles the pumpkin and supports its weight.

Pumpkins require a lot of water; be sure to keep the soil evenly moist. One week after blooms appear, side-dress the vines with fertilizer. (See page 37 for information on side-dressing.)

Like squash, pumpkins depend on bees to pollinate the blossoms. If bees are not active in your garden, pollinate the flowers yourself by transferring pollen from male to female flowers with an artist's brush. Fruit will not form without pollination. You can identify the female flowers by the swollen base of the blossom stem.

Harvest and Storage

Pumpkins are ready for harvest when the vines die and the fruit turns a rich orange or the color typical of the selection. If you can pierce the skin with your thumbnail, the fruit is immature. Although yields vary according to selection, weather, and cultural conditions, you can usually expect to harvest three to four pumpkins per plant. Large-fruited selections may yield only one or two fruit per plant.

Cut the pumpkins from the vines, leaving 3 inches of stem attached. Handle pumpkins carefully to avoid bruising or scarring them. Fruit with broken stems or punctured skin will rot in storage, as will fruit that is harvested after a frost.

Pumpkins must be cured before they can be stored. To cure, place them in a well-ventilated, warm (75 to 85 degrees) location for one or two weeks.

Pumpkins are ready for harvest when the vines begin to die.

Different Selections

Popular Halloween pumpkins include Connecticut Field, a vigorous vine plant and prolific producer that will supply 15-pound, bright orange pumpkins whose flesh may be used for pies. Spooktacular is a small, deep orange pumpkin with a classic jack-o'-lantern shape. For a Halloween surprise, try Lumina, which bears white fruit that weighs 10 to 12 pounds and keeps well.

Good pumpkins for cooking include Small Sugar, a traditional favorite for home gardens; it produces round 6- to 8-pound fruit with dry, sweet flesh. Baby Bear, an All-America Selections winner, produces 2-pound pumpkins with fine flesh for pies and edible seeds for toasting; it is tolerant of fusarium wilt and gummy stem blight.

In small gardens where space is limited, choose Bushkin or Spirit; both hybrids grow compact 5- to 6-foot vines and produce small to medium-sized pumpkins that are good for carving. For charming, decorative pumpkins, plant Jack Be Little, which yields miniature orange fruit. Baby Boo is a white version of the same size fruit.

Troubleshooting

Pumpkins are sensitive to leaf spots, fusarium wilt, anthracnose, mildews, and gummy stem blight. As a preventive measure, choose disease-resistant selections or hardy heirlooms. Pumpkins can also attract vine borers, cucumber beetles, and squash bugs. See pages 120, 121, and 123 for more about these pests. You may wish to plant several crops in succession to try out different selections.

The size of the flowers of a pumpkin vine foreshadow the size of the fruit to follow.

Radishes

Short-crop radishes are best harvested in early spring when the roots are ¾ to 1½ inches in diameter.

Radishes make their way from the ground to the kitchen table in just three to four weeks, and can be enjoyed through three seasons. Radishes also come in an array of shapes and colors, and cover a range of flavors, from sweet and mild to peppery and hot.

Planting and Care

Radishes are grown from seed in spring, fall, and winter. Sow small amounts of seed every 10 days for a steady supply, rather than raising one large crop.

For spring, grow **short-crop** radishes, that is, radishes that mature in a very short time, usually 21 to 30 days. Begin planting two to four weeks before the last frost and continue planting until four weeks after it. These crispy, mild radishes are ideal for interplanting with other crops, particularly those that are slow to germinate, such as carrots. They also grow well in containers.

For fall, you can plant short-crop radishes again, four to six weeks before the first frost. Or you can plant **midseason** radishes, which take longer to mature—about 45 to 60 days. These radishes, also called Oriental and Daikon radishes, include selections that produce long, firm roots like carrots; they have a mild flavor and tolerate hotter weather better than short-crop types. Plant in late summer, about eight weeks before the first frost.

For winter, grow **long-season** radishes, also called winter radishes. They require 55 to 70 days to mature and are larger and firmer than short-crop radishes. Their crisp, mildly pungent flesh keeps well in storage. Sow seeds at least four weeks before the first frost.

Radishes need loose, well-drained soil so that they can develop rapidly; if they grow slowly, the roots will be tough and stunted. If your soil is heavy clay, amend it or plant radishes in raised beds. (Long-rooted selections do especially well in raised beds.) Radishes perform best in soil with a pH between 6.0 and 6.8 but will tolerate a pH as low as 5.5. Before sowing, work fertilizer into the soil.

Sow short-crop radishes in rows 6 to 12 inches apart, and cover seeds with ½ inch of soil. Space rows for midseason radishes 10 to 15 inches apart, and sow seeds ¾ inch deep. Sow long-season radishes at

---

AT A GLANCE
❖
RADISHES

Season: cool weather

Days to harvest: 21 to 70

Plant size: 6 to 8 inches tall, 4 to 6 inches wide

Final spacing: *short-crop:* plants, 2 inches; rows, 6 to 12 inches; *midseason:* plants, 3 to 5 inches; rows, 10 to 15 inches; *long-season:* plants, 6 inches; rows, 18 to 20 inches

Soil: loose, well drained, pH 5.5 to 6.8

Water: medium

Pests: none specific

Remarks: thinning is important

the same depth, but space rows 18 to 20 inches apart. Thin plants soon after they emerge, as crowding prevents good roots from forming. Thin short-crop radishes to 2 inches, midseason radishes to 3 to 5 inches, and long-season radishes to 6 inches. If you sow seeds over a wide row, thin to the same spacing. Keep the soil evenly moist. Excessive or uneven moisture may cause radishes to split or become overly hot.

Harvest and Storage

Short-crop radishes are ready to harvest when they are ¾ to 1½ inches in diameter. Do not leave short-crop radishes in the ground too long after they reach harvesting size because they will become oversized, hot, and tough.

Pull midseason selections when the roots are 6 to 12 inches long. Harvest long-season types when the roots are about 3 inches in diameter. Both types usually push out of the ground about an inch when they are ready to be harvested. Midseason and long-season types can be left in the ground for several weeks after they mature without becoming tough. Long-season selections withstand light frost.

To store, trim tops close to the root and put the radishes in the refrigerator. They will keep one to four months, depending on the selection.

Different Selections

Short-crop selections include the ever-dependable Cherry Belle, a classic round, red radish, and French Breakfast, an oblong red. For fun, try Easter Egg; a single packet of seeds will produce crunchy radishes in purple, red, and white. White Icicle will have oblong white roots up to 5 inches long. Snow Belle has round, white roots. Midseason selections include Oriental radishes such as Summer Cross Hybrid, which develops long, carrot-shaped white roots that may stretch to 1 foot long in deep, loose soil. April Cross is similar but grows to 18 inches. Long-season selections include German Beer, named after the German custom of cutting radishes into thin slices and serving them as appetizers with draft beer; and Long Black Spanish, a 10-inch-long black radish that is very tolerant of cold weather.

Troubleshooting

Radishes grow so fast that they have few pest problems. If insects attack, pick them off by hand or pull up the affected plants.

Radishes are attractive in a kitchen garden when planted with other cool-season plants, such as onions and pansies.

Because short-crop radishes mature in only 21 to 30 days, you can sow them between later-maturing crops, such as cabbage.

Spinach

A small planting of tender spinach will thrive in cool weather.

Spinach is both easy to grow and small enough to be raised in tiny gardens and containers. Even a small planting yields an abundance of tender leaves for salads, soups, and soufflés in spring and fall. Fast-growing, spinach can be harvested within five or six weeks of planting. It is especially sweet after a frost.

Planting and Care

You can grow spinach in early spring and again in fall. In spring, start seeds early, four to six weeks before the last frost. Late-planted spinach bolts quickly as days become longer, and leaves acquire a strong, bitter flavor. Spinach may also bolt if planted near streetlights, floodlights, or other night lighting.

For fall and winter harvests, plant seeds four to eight weeks before the first frost. Be sure to plant enough to last through winter; although growth stops when cold weather arrives, plants will survive freezing temperatures. Leave them in the garden and harvest as needed through winter. To protect plants from severe weather, cover them with a light mulch, such as pine straw. As temperatures rise in spring, young plants that overwintered will begin growing again and will give you an early harvest. However, because these plants are already mature, they will bolt with the first warm spell.

Spinach likes rich, organic soil with a pH of 6.0 to 6.8. Before planting, work fertilizer into the soil. Sow seeds thinly (¼ inch deep) in rows spaced 1½ feet apart, or scatter seeds over a wide bed. Cover with ½ inch of soil. Thin seedlings to 4 to 6 inches apart; thinning is important because crowding stunts the plants' growth. Keep the bed evenly moist, especially while seeds are germinating.

In warm weather, you can grow New Zealand spinach, a spinach substitute that produces until the first hard freeze. New Zealand spinach looks and tastes almost like true spinach when it is cooked. It grows on a vining stem, spreading to 4 feet, and can be trained up a trellis or a thin stake. Although the plants grow in warm weather, the seeds need cooler soil to germinate; plant in early to midspring. Or start seeds indoors four to six weeks before the last frost. To help speed germination, soak the seeds overnight before planting. Sow seeds 1 inch deep in rows 3 feet apart. Each seed is actually a cluster of seeds from which several seedlings germinate, so be sure to thin early to a spacing of 1 to 1½ feet.

AT A GLANCE

❖

SPINACH

Season: cool weather

Days to harvest: 35 to 70

Plant size: 6 to 10 inches tall, 4 to 6 inches wide

Final spacing: plants, 4 to 6 inches; rows, 1 to 1½ feet

Soil: rich, organic, pH 6.0 to 6.8

Water: medium

Pests: flea beetles, aphids, spider mites, downy mildew, white rust

Remarks: fall crop is the best, will tolerate freezing weather

New Zealand spinach, a good warm-weather substitute for true spinach, is a short vine that will wrap around a trellis or a tomato stake.

Harvest and Storage

There are two ways to harvest spinach. You can pinch off just the large outer leaves when they are 3 to 6 inches long, allowing the plant to produce new leaves from its center. (This briefly delays bolting in spring.) Or you can cut the entire plant at soil level when it reaches 4 to 6 inches in diameter.

When New Zealand spinach plants are 6 to 9 inches tall, begin harvesting by pinching about 3 inches of each branch tip. This encourages more branching and new growth. As plants continue to branch, you can increase the amount you harvest. However, growth will stop if you cut the plant back or pinch out the top.

All spinach will keep two weeks in the refrigerator, but do not wash the leaves until you are ready to use them.

Different Selections

For a spring planting, choose selections that are heat tolerant and slow to bolt, such as Bloomsdale Long Standing, Avon, Italian Summer, Tyee Hybrid, or Estivato. In fall, look for selections with disease resistance and cold hardiness, such as Melody Hybrid, Winter Bloomsdale, Bloomsdale Long Standing, Early Hybrid No. 7, Chesapeake, or Dixie Market.

Savoyed (crinkle-leafed) selections have more leaf surface than smooth-leafed types, so they produce more food per planting. But savoyed selections can also be more difficult to clean because soil lodges in the curls and crevices. You may want to mulch these plants to help keep them cleaner.

Mulch helps keep these savoyed spinach clean by preventing soil from splashing on the undersides of the leaves.

Troubleshooting

Flea beetles, aphids, and spider mites feed on spinach leaves. See pages 120 and 122 for more about these pests. Downy mildew and white rust can also be problems. Downy mildew will ruin plants in cool, moist weather; choose selections such as Melody Hybrid or Winter Bloomsdale, which are resistant. White rust is a disease that causes white spots on the foliage.

Squash

Summer squash comes in many shapes: long, round, and scalloped.

AT A GLANCE
❖
SUMMER SQUASH

Season: warm weather

Days to harvest: 35 to 60

Plant size: bush: 3 feet tall, 4 feet wide; vining: 2 feet tall, 6 feet long

Final spacing: 2 plants per hill; hills, 3 feet

Soil: well drained, pH 5.5 to 6.8

Water: medium

Pests: squash vine borers, cucumber beetles, squash bugs, anthracnose, mildews

Remarks: pest control is critical to success

Squash is one of the most productive vegetables in the garden. There are two types of squash: the fast-growing, tender summer squash and the slower-growing, sweet, meaty winter squash. Planted in spring, summer squash is ready for the first harvest by early summer. Winter squash takes a month or two longer, but it is worth the wait because of the variety it adds to the late summer and fall harvest.

Planting and Care

Summer and winter squash require the same care and cultural conditions. They prefer organic, well-drained soil with a pH between 6.0 and 6.8 but find soil with a pH of 5.5 tolerable. Work in fertilizer before sowing seeds. Squash is usually planted in hills spaced 3 feet apart (from the center of each hill). Plants depend on bees to pollinate the flowers, so for better pollination and fruiting, plant two rows of hills side by side instead of one long row.

Sow five to seven seeds per hill after danger of frost has passed, planting them 1 inch deep. After the seedlings have been up about one week, thin to the two strongest plants per hill. Crowded plants produce less fruit and are more likely to develop diseases.

Troubleshooting

Squash are susceptible to insects such as squash vine borers, cucumber beetles, squash bugs, anthracnose, and mildews. See pages 120–124 for more about these pests and diseases.

Summer Squash

The three most popular types of summer squash are yellow (crookneck and straightneck), zucchini, and pattypan (scalloped). Most selections are bush types, which produce short vines. Regularly picking the soft-skinned, immature fruit keeps it coming for eight weeks or longer.

Plant summer squash immediately after the last frost. Plant again three weeks later to extend the harvest. A third planting in midsummer will give you late summer and fall harvests, but be prepared to control insect pests as soon as seedlings emerge.

Harvest and Storage

Summer squash quickly reach harvest size in three to seven days after the flowers open. Pick yellow squash when they are 4 to 6 inches long, zucchini when 6 to 8 inches long, and pattypan types when 3 to 5 inches in diameter. If the rind is hard, the fruit is overripe. It should be picked and added to the compost. Leaving fruit on the plants until they are overmature will slow production.

Summer squash will keep in the refrigerator one to two weeks.

Different Selections

Yellow Crookneck, an heirloom selection, produces plentiful fruit that is best picked when 6 inches long or shorter. Sundance is a hybrid early crookneck that yields an abundance of bright yellow, smooth-skinned fruit. Goldbar is a hearty producer of straight-necked yellow squash; Early Prolific Straightneck lives up to its name.

For variety, try the scalloped pattypan types of summer squash. Sunburst Hybrid yields bright yellow scalloped fruit. Sun Drops Hybrid produces miniature, oval-shaped, creamy yellow fruit. Peter Pan Hybrid will keep you supplied with apple green pattypan squash, which are grown on runnerless plants. All three hybrids are All-America Selections winners. Scallopini Hybrid is also worth trying.

There are many zucchini selections to choose from. Cocozelle or Dark Green has long, cylindrical green fruits. Gold Rush Hybrid, an All-America Selections winner, produces glossy, golden fruit, as does Golden Dawn II Hybrid. Gourmet Globe and Roly Poly Hybrids offer globe-shaped zucchini that are 4 to 6 inches in diameter and well suited for stuffing.

Winter Squash

In contrast to summer squash, winter squash produces only one major harvest. But the hard-skinned, mature fruit can be stored for several months, so you can enjoy them throughout fall and winter. Popular winter squash include acorn, butternut, and the extra-large Hubbard.

Make a spring planting immediately after the last frost for a midsummer harvest. A second planting in early to midsummer will be ready for harvest in late fall.

Although many winter squash are vining plants that need more garden space than summer squash, bush and semibush selections of acorn and butternut squash are also available. Plant these in hills spaced 3 to 4 feet apart. Plant vining selections of acorn and butternut squash in hills spaced 4 to 5 feet apart. These types produce fruit that weigh 1 to 4 pounds.

Large vining types of winter squash, such as Pink Banana and Hubbard, bear fruit weighing 12 to 15 pounds or more. They require 5 to 7 feet between hills.

A vining winter squash makes a good companion to upright corn.

AT A GLANCE
❖
WINTER SQUASH

Season: warm weather
Days to harvest: 50 to 120
Plant size: bush: 3 feet tall, 4 feet wide; vining: 2 feet tall, 6 to 12 feet long
Final spacing: bush: 2 plants per hill; hills, 3 to 4 feet; vining: 2 plants per hill; hills, 4 to 5 feet
Soil: well drained, pH 5.5 to 6.8
Water: medium
Pests: squash vine borers, cucumber beetles, and others
Remarks: choose bush types for small gardens

Bush types of both winter and summer squash are best for small gardens.

Harvest and Storage

Of the winter squash, only acorn squash can be harvested and enjoyed before it is fully mature. Other winter squash selections must be fully mature to have a sweet flavor. Fruit is ready to harvest when you are unable to pierce the skin with your thumbnail. Often the plants have started to turn yellow and die back. Cut the squash from the vine, leaving 2 to 3 inches of stem attached. Before storing, cure as you would pumpkins. (See page 103 for more about curing.)

Winter squash will keep one to three months, depending upon the selection. Store squash in a cool, dry place, such as a garage or basement.

Different Selections

Winter squash selections vary greatly in size and appearance, but most are grown for their sweet, meaty flesh. Spaghetti squash, however, has a stringy center and is used as a low-calorie substitute for pasta.

If you have space, try vining types such as Waltham Butternut, which produces uniform, dark orange fruits with good flavor. Early Butternut Hybrid, an All-America Selections winner, bears tan, sweet fruit on more compact vines. Pink Banana produces cylindrical 36-inch-long fruit that turns a pinkish orange when ripe. Blue Hubbard bears 15-pound blue, ridged fruit with a sweet flesh prized for freezing.

For smaller gardens, grow bush types. The acorn selection Table King produces a dark green fruit with golden flesh. The fruit of Burpee's Bush is similar to that of Table King and is excellent for baking. (There is also a vining type called Table Queen.) Cream of the Crop, an All-America Selections winner, produces 3-pound golden acorn squash with delicious, nutty-flavored creamy white flesh. All Seasons Hybrid is an early-maturing bush-type butternut that produces small, sweet fruit in just 50 days.

Swiss Chard

Lush leaves marked with striking, colorful ribs make Swiss chard as much an ornamental as a gourmet delicacy. Despite its glamorous appearance, Swiss chard tolerates more summer heat than other greens and grows through fall until killed by a hard freeze.

Planting and Care

A single planting in spring will give you harvests until early winter. But leaves are sweeter and more tender in early spring and fall when temperatures are cool. For spring and summer harvests, you may plant in spring, two to four weeks before the last frost. For fall harvests, plant in summer, 10 to 12 weeks before the first frost.

Although you may start Swiss chard from transplants, direct seeding is easier. Soak seeds overnight to speed germination. Swiss chard grows best in average soil with a pH between 6.0 and 6.8. Work fertilizer into the soil before planting.

Sow seed in wide beds or in single rows spaced 1 to 1½ feet apart. The seed is actually clusters of seeds that will produce several plants. When plants are 1 inch tall, thin each cluster to one plant every 3 to 4 inches. When plants grow large enough to touch each other, thin to one plant every 9 to 12 inches. Or set out transplants 9 to 12 inches apart at the same time you would sow seeds.

Water regularly, as drought-stressed plants may bolt.

Harvest and Storage

Harvest outer leaves when they are just large enough to eat; young, tender leaves are more flavorful. In fall, harvest before a hard freeze.

Swiss chard will keep two weeks in the refrigerator.

Different Selections

Try red-stemmed selections such as Ruby Red, which stands out with its crimson stalks and crinkled leaves.

For white-stemmed selections, consider Fordhook Giant, which has heavy yields of dark green leaves even in hot weather; Lucullus Light Green, the most popular Swiss chard, is appreciated for its smooth leaves. Geneva is more winter hardy than most selections.

Troubleshooting

Swiss chard can have problems with cercospora leaf spot and downy mildew. See page 124 for more about these diseases. Look for selections resistant to these diseases.

Swiss chard is one of the more ornamental vegetables.

AT A GLANCE
SWISS CHARD

Season: cool and warm weather

Days to harvest: 55 to 60

Plant size: 2 feet tall, 1½ feet wide

Final spacing: plants, 9 to 12 inches; rows, 18 to 24 inches

Soil: average, pH 6.0 to 6.8

Water: medium

Pests: cercospora leaf spot, downy mildew

Remarks: one of the most heat-tolerant greens

Tomatoes

A ripe tomato will be firm and brightly colored with a little green at the stem end.

If there is one vegetable that guarantees success measured by the pound, it is the tomato. Its prolific production of fruit with unbeatable flavor makes it the most popular vegetable to grow. And while tomatoes are easy to raise, the plants require a lot of attention because they may remain in the garden from spring until frost.

Planting and Care

Plant tomatoes in spring after the danger of frost has passed. The easiest way to start tomatoes is from purchased transplants, but for hard-to-find heirlooms or unusual selections, you will probably have to grow your own transplants from seed.

There are many methods of planting tomatoes, but all have one step in common: plant deeply in well-amended soil. Tomatoes are heavy feeders and like rich, well-drained soil with a pH between 6.0 and 6.8; however, they find a pH of 5.5 tolerable. Before planting, work plenty of compost or other organic matter into the soil. In calcium-deficient soils, you may need to add dolomitic lime in the fall, before a spring planting. This will help prevent blossom end rot. (Turn to page 125 for a description of this disease.)

You may fertilize tomatoes by working slow-release fertilizer into the soil before planting. Some gardeners prefer to use liquid tomato food, fertilizing every two weeks from the time transplants are first set out until they begin bearing heavily. Be careful not to overfertilize, however, or you will have abundant foliage but few tomatoes.

Set short, stocky plants deep enough so that the lowest leaf is about 2 inches above the ground. For tall, leggy plants, strip all but the top 2 to 4 inches of the stem and lay the plant sideways in a trench 2 to 3 inches deep. Cover with soil, keeping the leafy portion above ground. Roots will form along the buried stem, creating a stronger root system. Firm the soil around the plant, and fertilize with a starter solution. Two to three weeks after planting, mulch heavily to keep down weeds and conserve soil moisture.

The distance at which you set tomato plants depends on how they are supported. Plant tomatoes in cages 3 feet apart; plant tomatoes that are to be supported by a trellis or stakes 1 to 2 feet apart in rows 3 to 4 feet apart.

Water plants regularly so that the soil stays evenly moist. Letting the soil dry out and then soaking it can cause blossom drop or cracks in the fruit and will contribute to blossom end rot. Avoid getting foliage wet during watering, as this promotes disease. Lay a hose at the base of the plant and let the water run gently, or use a soaker hose or a drip irrigation system.

Once tomato plants are about 3 feet tall, you can root **suckers** for additional plantings. Suckers grow at the junction of the main stem and a leaf branch. Cut off 3- to 4-inch-long suckers, remove the leaves from the lower half, and insert each stem in a pot filled with sterile potting soil. Set the pots in a well-lit place but out of direct sunlight, and keep the soil evenly moist until new growth appears, indicating that roots are formed. Rooting suckers in midsummer is a good way to start plants for the fall garden.

Support Structures for Tomatoes

Tomato plants need support to keep their branches off the ground. If they are permitted to sprawl, they become more susceptible to diseases and take up more space. Support structures include stakes, trellises, and wire cages. Stakes are temporary and inexpensive solutions, especially suitable for short selections. Trellises are equally quick and simple and are good for vining tomatoes. Wire cages are more expensive, but they involve less work, as shoots do not have to be tied as they do to a stake or trellis.

Whether to stake, cage, or trellis depends on personal preference and the growth habit of the plant. Bush tomatoes, which are called **determinate** types, are shorter and bushier than vining types. Most determinate types grow 3 to 4 feet tall, require minimal support, and seldom need pruning. Determinate tomato plants ripen most of their fruit over a short period, which makes them especially convenient for canning or drying. To extend the harvest from early summer until fall, plant determinate selections with staggered maturity dates. Or stretch the harvest season into fall by planting three times: mid-spring, early summer, and late summer.

Vining tomatoes, which are called **indeterminate,** can grow from 5 to 12 feet tall, depending on the selection. The most popular type of tomato, they grow and bear fruit continuously until frost. Indeterminate types require ample support and frequent pruning to keep offshoots (which need to be tied up) to a manageable number. Prune weekly, but do not remove a lot of foliage all at once or you may expose fruit to the sun, which causes sunscald and uneven ripening.

Tomato plants need a stake or other support to keep the fruit off the ground.

GROWING WHOPPERS

Beefsteak tomatoes are trickier to grow than small tomatoes because they take longer to reach full size. Many are also heirloom tomatoes and therefore not as disease resistant as new, improved selections. Here are some tips for growing prizewinning whoppers.

• Grow your own transplants so you can choose the largest, strongest selections.

• Space plants farther apart than you would smaller-fruited types.

• Use super-rich organic soil; supplement with a liquid tomato food until plants begin bearing.

• Water evenly to keep the skin of the fruit from cracking.

• Prune each plant to one or two stems, unless instructions for the particular selection indicate otherwise.

• As fruit appears, pick immature tomatoes from the top of the plant, leaving only a few whopper candidates below that are closest to the main stem.

When frost threatens, pick green tomatoes and store them in a cool, dry place.

Meaty Roma tomatoes are preferred for sauces and pastes.

Harvest and Storage

A ripe tomato is firm and brightly colored and a little bit green at the stem end. It will remain in good condition on the vine for about two days before starting to deteriorate. If it is soft or deeply colored, or if the skin is crinkly, the tomato is overripe. Use it for juice or fresh salsa but not for canning. Store ripe tomatoes at room temperature, above 60 degrees. Do not refrigerate as this causes rapid deterioration.

To use green tomatoes still on the vine in late fall, pick them just before frost. Tomatoes that are whitish green and have formed a corky ring where the stem joins the fruit will ripen slowly indoors. Store on shelves in a cool location, above 50 degrees, for several weeks. To keep them even longer, wrap green tomatoes individually in newspaper, place them in a basket, greenest on the bottom, and put the basket in a cool, dark place, such as a basement. Check occasionally for ripe or spoiled fruit. A quick way to store tomatoes when frost is approaching is to pull up the whole plant and hang it upside down in a dark, cool place.

Different Selections

Tomatoes are region specific. A selection that grows well in the Midwest may do poorly in the deep South, where warm night temperatures may cause blossoms to drop or where different pests and diseases are common. Your local nursery growers or county Extension agent will know of area favorites.

Unless you are willing to nurse temperamental tomatoes, look for disease-resistant or disease-tolerant selections. The initials F or FF, N, T, or V after the name indicate resistance or tolerance to the most common tomato problems: fusarium wilt (races 1 or 2), nematodes, Tobacco Mosaic Virus, and verticillium wilt. Some heirloom selections are not rated for resistance but may be problem free.

Also consider your purpose for growing tomatoes. If you want a large, sweet slicing tomato for sandwiches, choose a beefsteak. For cooking, choose a selection such as Roma, which has a rich flavor and meaty texture that is better suited for sauces. The flavor of a tomato is due to the balance of acidity, sweetness, and aroma. Differences in acidity between tomato selections are minor and depend primarily on climate, soil, cultural practices, and ripeness.

For sweet cherry tomatoes, try Super Sweet 100 VF, a disease-resistant, indeterminate tomato. The heirloom Gardener's Delight is another indeterminate that produces clusters of 6 to 12 tomatoes all summer. For small yellow tomatoes, try Sun Gold, an indeterminate, which bears fruit that ripens early into grapelike clusters of tasty golden tomatoes; or another indeterminate, Yellow Pear, which produces abundant juicy, pale orange tomatoes. All cherry tomatoes are heavy producers, even in hot weather.

Selections that produce medium-sized fruit include Celebrity VFFNT, a determinate All-America Selections winner. Enchantment VFFNT produces egg-shaped fruit with full-bodied flavor on an indeterminate vine. Early Girl produces early and continues throughout the summer on indeterminate vines. Heat Wave is a determinate hybrid, a member of the so-called "heat-set" tomatoes that keep producing even when daytime temperatures reach the 90s. Better Bush Improved VFF forms a sturdy, 4-foot plant that is excellent for containers.

For large beefsteak tomatoes, try Brandywine, an indeterminate that many gardeners consider to have set the taste standard. Big Beef VFFTN, an indeterminate All-America Selections winner, is disease resistant and adapts well to many regions, producing fruits 12 ounces or larger. Better Boy VFN is an old standby indeterminate with excellent yields. The heirloom Radiator Charlie's Mortgage Lifter produces fruit averaging more than 1 pound on indeterminate vines; it sometimes yields 4-pound prizewinners.

For novelty tomatoes, try Husky Gold Hybrid, a determinate All-America Selections winner that produces 7- to 8-ounce golden fruit with exceptionally flavorful flesh of the same color. For a conversation piece, grow the unusual orange-colored heirloom Persimmon, an indeterminate type. Green Zebra is an indeterminate selection that ripens from light green to golden amber with deep green stripes. It tastes both sweet and tart at the same time.

If you want to make tomato paste or other concentrated tomato products, consider the heirloom San Marzano, an indeterminate, or Roma VF, a determinate. Viva Italia FVN is a determinate that is an excellent choice for sauces and soups; it also grows well in hot weather.

Troubleshooting

Tomatoes, especially those grown in warm climates, are prone to disease. Choosing disease-resistant selections or hardy heirlooms is critical to success.

Insects such as stinkbugs, spider mites, flea beetles, cutworms, potato beetles, and aphids enjoy dining on tomatoes and their foliage. The leaf-eating tomato hornworm can completely strip a plant in 48 hours or less. For more about these pests, see pages 120–123.

Pear tomato plants produce clusters of lovely fruit with a rich tomato flavor.

Plant different tomato selections for a harvest rich in variety.

Turnips

A harvest of turnips is always best in early spring and in fall when the weather is cool.

Turnips are hearty vegetables whose roots are often enjoyed in winter soups and stews. However, turnips are grown for their greens as well. Traditionally boiled and eaten with hot sauce or pepper vinegar, turnip greens are a favorite crop for spring and are even tastier in fall, when light frosts sweeten the leaves. Colder temperatures also improve the flavor of the white, yellow, or purple roots.

Planting and Care

Turnips require cool weather. Once daytime temperatures are consistently above 80 degrees, the greens turn strong and bitter and the roots become stringy and woody. For spring harvests, plant four weeks before the last frost. For fall and winter harvests, plant again in late summer or early fall.

Turnips prefer fertile, loose, well-drained soil with a pH between 6.0 and 6.8 but find a pH as low as 5.5 tolerable. Fertilize and till the soil before planting. In infertile heavy clay or rocky soils, the roots will be tough, woody, and possibly misshapen because their growth will be stunted.

You can grow turnips either in wide beds or in conventional rows spaced 15 to 18 inches apart. After working fertilizer into the soil, sow seeds thinly and cover with ½ inch of soil. Water well to ensure germination. Thin seedlings to 1 to 3 inches apart if you are primarily interested in greens; thin to 6 inches apart for good-sized roots. To extend harvests, make two or three sowings two weeks apart. Harvesting tops frequently stunts the growth of the roots; plant enough to allow for harvesting of both tops and roots.

To produce tender, sweet roots, turnips need to grow steadily and receive regular waterings. Plants harvested for greens also need extra fertilizer to continue producing foliage. You should mulch to keep roots moist in warm weather and to protect from cold in the fall.

Harvest and Storage

To harvest turnip greens, pinch off the older outer leaves at the base or cut off all of them with a knife. (The plant will produce new ones.) Leaves taste best when they are 2 to 10 inches long; older ones tend to be tough and strongly flavored.

Pull roots when they are about 2 to 3 inches in diameter; if any larger, they may be bitter. Roots tolerate frost, so you can leave them in the ground and dig as needed, especially if the plants are well mulched. Alternate freezing and thawing, however, may affect the

---

AT A GLANCE

❖

TURNIPS

Season: cool weather

Days to harvest: greens, 27 to 45; roots, 35 to 75

Plant size: 12 to 20 inches tall, 12 inches wide

Final spacing: plants, 1 to 3 inches for greens, 6 inches for roots; rows, 15 to 18 inches

Soil: fertile, loose, well drained, pH 5.5 to 6.8

Water: medium

Pests: downy mildew, leaf spot, flea beetles, aphids

Remarks: best planted in late summer for fall harvest

quality of the roots. It is best to harvest them before the first hard freeze.

To store turnips, trim tops to within 1 inch of the root and refrigerate; they will keep two to four weeks. Greens will keep two weeks in the refrigerator. The old-fashioned method for storing turnips is to pack them in damp sand (cover completely and be sure they do not touch), and store in a cool, humid location, such as a basement. If you choose this method, first trim away tops and part of the *taproot,* the long thin root at the tip of the turnip. The turnips will stay fresh for several months.

Different Selections

Purple Top White Globe is an old standby that produces sweet, fine-grained turnips that are white with a purple band. Its relative, Royal Crown Hybrid, produces creamy white roots and thick leaves. White Egg is a fast-growing turnip that is popular in warmer areas. Both the roots and tops of Just Right Hybrid have excellent flavor. Tokyo Cross Hybrid is a white All-America Selections winner that is recommended for spring crops.

For greens only, Shogoin is a hardy selection that tolerates hot, dry weather, resists aphids, and still provides a heavy yield of tender, mild greens. Alamo is disease tolerant and produces greens that are similar in flavor to mustard greens or spinach. All Top Hybrid replaces greens quickly after they are cut and is slow to bolt. And Seven Top, an heirloom and enduring favorite in warmer regions, can be grown as a winter annual.

Troubleshooting

If turnips develop hollow or gray-brown cores, there may be a boron deficiency in the soil. Have the soil tested for trace elements and amend according to recommendations. Turnips are also attacked by downy mildew and leaf spots; if these diseases are problems in your area, choose resistant selections. Also watch out for flea beetles and aphids. Turn to pages 120–122 for more about these insects.

Turnips are frequently grown for their sweet greens, which can be harvested a month after planting.

117

Pest and Disease Control

The photographs and descriptions on these pages will help you recognize harmful insects and diseases. Some pests, once established, are difficult to control. However, insects such as ladybugs (adults and larvae), green lacewings, and certain wasps prey on pests that are damaging to your crops.

Integrated Pest Management

The most sensible approach to pest control is called Integrated Pest Management, or IPM. This strategy encourages you to reduce spraying by 1) checking the garden weekly for pests; 2) identifying pests and assessing the damage; 3) deciding if the damage is tolerable or if the potential for more damage calls for control measures to save the harvest.

For example, a corn earworm likes to nibble on the tip of the ear where the corn is tasseling. But if you spray pesticides to prevent or eliminate the earworm, you may eliminate honeybees as well. If you reconcile yourself to slicing off the tip of the ear of corn after you harvest it, there is no need for control.

Your local Extension agent is a good source for materials on IPM, which also includes the wise use of pesticides.

Gardening Practices That Reduce Insects

One way to prevent or reduce insect problems is to manage the garden in a way that discourages them. These are some practices that will help minimize problems.

• **Turn the soil in winter.** Turn or till the soil several times in winter (when the soil is not soggy) to expose insects to freezing weather. This will help kill insects such as corn earworm and cutworm that overwinter in the soil before reproducing in spring.

• **Plant early and use resistant selections.** Many pests migrate into gardens as temperatures rise in spring and summer. Therefore, their numbers are lower on early-planted crops. Late-season crops, especially summer transplants grown for planting in the fall, are the hardest hit. Use row covers or vegetable selections developed to resist certain insects.

• **Start with certified plants and seeds.** Some insects, such as sweet potato weevils, may be found with the seeds or plants purchased to start the crop. To prevent problems with pests and diseases, use only certified plants or seeds.

• **Space plants properly.** Crowding makes it easier for foliage-feeding insects to move from plant to plant, so space your plants appropriately.

• **Rotate crops.** Insects that spend part of their life cycle in the soil will build up in the soil if the same vegetable is grown in the same place year after year. Crop rotation helps reduce the number of Colorado potato beetles, for example.

• **Cultivate beneficial bugs.** Some insects, such as ladybugs and lacewings, are natural predators of insects that feed on vegetables. They will appear in your garden when the pests they feed on are there but may move or die if they have nothing to eat. And be aware that certain pesticides will kill both pest and predator.

• **Clean up after harvest.** Always remove plants as soon as the crop is harvested. Dead plants provide shelter in winter for squash bugs, Mexican bean beetles, European corn borers, and other insects that will emerge and breed again in spring.

Gardening Practices That Reduce Diseases

Plant selections resistant to or tolerant of diseases. Resistant plants do not become infected, while tolerant selections may be mildly affected, but will continue to produce. When possible, time plantings to avoid the months that diseases are most active. Call your local Extension agent for the best planting times and for information on resistant selections.

• **Rotate crops.** Do not grow vegetables that are susceptible to the same diseases in the same spot every season. Move these crops at least 10 feet each year. For example, black rot attacks cabbage, collards, kale, and broccoli. Do not grow any of these plants in the same spot more often than every three years.

• **Thin and space properly.** Thinning seedlings and setting transplants at the proper spacing help prevent disease by allowing good air circulation, which keeps the foliage dry. Crowded plants stay wet longer, thus inviting disease.

• **Water plants in the morning.** Watering at night gives fungi a head start on development by keeping foliage wet for an extended length of time. It is best to water very early in the morning before the dew dries.

• **Mulch with care.** Keep mulches an inch or two away from the base of plants. Mulching too close keeps moisture next to the stem and encourages disease.

• **Destroy all infected plants immediately.** Leaving them in the garden ensures reinfection later. Garden cleanup of dead stalks and plant material helps prevent pests.

Pesticides

For safe and effective application of pesticides, always follow the directions on the label. Using pesticides in ways other than directed is against federal law.

Pesticides that control fungus diseases are called fungicides. Those that control insects are called insecticides. Pesticides are available in various forms, including dusts, sprays, baits, and granules. Sprays provide the best coverage and are least likely to weather away. To control insects, you must spray both sides of the leaves throroughly as many pests live or lay eggs on the underside of the leaves. Dusts are sprinkled on, often through holes in the pesticide container. Dusts are usually not as effective as sprays since they are quickly blown or washed away. Bees will inadvertently pick up dust on their bodies and carry it back to the hive where it can kill many bees. Bait and granular pesticides are usually formulated for insects that live in or near the soil.

Fungicides are available as sprays. To control fungus diseases, you must coat the foliage thoroughly. Fungicides need to be applied before a disease appears in order to prevent its rapid spread. It is therefore essential to learn what conditions favor particular diseases and to spray susceptible plants for diseases that you know appear in your garden each year.

PROTECT BEES FROM PESTICIDES

Many pesticides kill bees as well as pests. Without bees to pollinate blossoms, crops such as squash, melons, and cucumbers will not set fruit. Take the following precautions to reduce the danger to bees that are in your garden.

When you have a choice, select the pesticide least hazardous to bees, such as insecticidal soap. Most fungicides are also not harmful to bees. If you must use a pesticide that is toxic to bees, try to avoid applying it when a vegetable is in bloom and apply in the evening when bees are not active. Dusts and wettable powder sprays (a fine powder suspended in water) are more toxic to bees than other sprays.

Liquid concentrate formulas are generally better. To make your own insecticide soap spray, add a few drops of dish-washing detergent to water.

Insect Pests

Insects that commonly feed on vegetable plants fall into six major groups: beetles, caterpillars, aphids, true bugs, spider mites, and thrips. Understanding these groups is the first step in controlling these insects. When insects are large and few, simply pick them off with your gloved hands. In some cases you will need to spray the pests with water or an approved insecticide to prevent more damage. Contact your county Extension agent for a list of recommended pesticides.

The Chewing Insects

Beetles. Most beetles chew on flowers and foliage. The adults and larvae of Mexican bean beetles, for example, feed on foliage and can ruin plants by eating nearly all the leaves. Some species, such as sweet potato weevils, feed underground and cause damage to roots.

Asparagus beetle

Colorado potato beetle

Flea beetle

Mexican bean beetle larvae and adult

Pest	Description	Control
Asparagus beetle	black beetles with orange spots spend winter in protected places and feed on new shoots in spring; lay eggs on asparagus stems, where hungry larvae can defoliate a plant	during harvest season, remove volunteer plants and cut shoots just below soil surface so adults do not have a place to lay eggs; handpick or spray ferns with water or approved insecticide during cutting season; remove dead leaves in winter; ladybugs and some parasitic wasps feed on this pest
Blister beetle	large black beetles with yellow stripes feed on foliage of corn, tomatoes, and potatoes in early summer	handpick (wearing gloves), or shake to the ground and step on them; spray or dust foliage with approved insecticide
Colorado potato beetle	zebra-striped beetles spend winter underground and emerge in spring to lay eggs on leaves of potato plants; larvae feed on leaves; also attacks tomatoes	handpick beetles at first sign, or spray with approved insecticide
Cucumber beetle	small yellow-and-black beetles eat foliage of cucumbers, squash, and cantaloupe; appear in late spring; spread cucumber mosaic virus and bacterial cucumber wilt	protect young plants with row covers and uncover when blooms appear; spray foliage of older plants with approved insecticide
Flea beetle	small, dark beetles make perforations in foliage of corn, eggplant, potatoes, spinach, and sweet potatoes; jump like fleas when disturbed	spray or dust with approved insecticide; keep garden clean, as these insects overwinter in plant litter
Mexican bean beetle	black-spotted gold beetles shaped like ladybugs; appear in spring; multiply rapidly; will strip leaves of beans and Southern peas	handpick or cover underside of foliage with approved insecticide; repeat according to label directions; crush yellow egg clusters that appear on underside of leaves; plant beans early when beetles are few

Caterpillars. Caterpillars are the larvae of moths and butterflies. Most caterpillars chew on foliage; some species also feed or bore into fruit or stems with varying degrees of damage.

Pest	Description	Control
Cabbage looper	inchworm-type green caterpillars chew through outer leaves into head of cabbage	handpick or spray or dust with approved insecticide at first sign of presence
Imported cabbageworm	large gray-green, velvety caterpillars chew through outer leaves into head of cabbage	handpick or spray or dust with approved insecticide at first sign of presence
Corn earworm	striped green caterpillars feed on fine kernels at tip of corn ear; eggs are laid on corn silk	plant corn early, or use pest-resistant selections (with long husks that grow over tip of ear); or cut off damaged corn ear tips
Cutworm	curled, light or dark worms eat stems of plants near soil, especially new seedlings or transplants of tomatoes	protect transplants with collar made from 6-ounce plastic foam cup with bottom removed: slip cup over transplant and sink rim 1 inch into soil, leaving 1 to 2 inches above ground
European corn borer	young, fleshy caterpillars feed on corn in tassel in leaf whorl, beneath husks, or between ear and stalk in early summer; also infest stalks of beans, beets, peppers, and potatoes	crush white egg masses found on underside of corn leaves; spray with approved insecticide at first sign of infestation, before borers enter stalks and ears
Hornworm	plump, green worms with red or black hornlike growth on rear; a few hornworms can defoliate a full-sized tomato plant	handpick or spray with approved insecticide; hornworms covered with dozens of tiny white cocoons have been parasitized by beneficial wasps and should be left in garden
Pickleworm	white to green caterpillars emerge early in season; attack cucumber and squash by boring into fruits and stems	spray or dust with approved insecticide at first sign of worms in blossoms; repeat weekly; remove vines after harvest
Southern cornstalk borer	dingy white borers with brown spots infest cornstalks near ground; plants become twisted and shrunken	impossible to control once inside stalk; destroy corn plants after harvest, since insects overwinter in old stalks; turn soil in winter; rotate crops
Squash vine borer	white borers burrow into squash stems, causing plants to wilt; yellow excrement on stems shows where borers have entered	plant squash as soon as weather allows so plants will be producing before borers become numerous; difficult to control once inside stem except by splitting stem open horizontally and removing them; bury injured stem in compost

Cabbage looper

Corn earworm

Cutworm

Hornworm

The Sucking Insects

Aphids, Leafhoppers, Whiteflies. All of these insects pierce leaves and stems and suck plant sap so growth is stunted or the plant deformed. Many sucking insects produce a sticky, sweet excrement called *honeydew;* this attracts ants and encourages the growth of sooty mold, an unsightly but harmless black fungus. Some species of sucking insects transmit plant viruses, especially among late-planted crops.

Aphids

Whitefly larvae

Pest	Description	Control
Aphid	tiny, pear-shaped insects appear by hundreds on tender new growth and flower buds of all vegetables; may be green, yellow, brown, or black	spray at first sign of infestation with strong jet of water or with approved insecticide
Leafhopper	small, wedge-shaped green or yellow leaf-hoppers feed on stems and leaves of melons, tomatoes, and peppers; jump quickly when disturbed	spray pests with approved insecticide
Whitefly	larvae look like drops of clear wax on underside of leaves; adults look like tiny white moths and disperse in clouds if you disturb leaves	spray at first sign of infestation with an approved insecticide

Mites. Related to spiders, these eight-legged creatures are not insects (insects have six legs). Mites damage plants by sucking plant sap and can cause foliage to turn yellow or a crispy brown. They are worst in mild, dry weather and will disappear during rainy periods or hot spells.

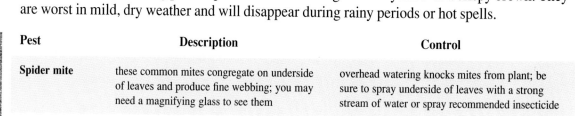

Spider mite damage

Pest	Description	Control
Spider mite	these common mites congregate on underside of leaves and produce fine webbing; you may need a magnifying glass to see them	overhead watering knocks mites from plant; be sure to spray underside of leaves with a strong stream of water or spray recommended insecticide

Thrips. Thrips are very small, slender, torpedo-shaped insects. They suck plant sap, causing white blotching on the leaves. Thrips are also attracted to flower blossoms; feeding there may deform fruit or stop its development.

Onion thrip

Pest	Description	Control
Thrip	first signs of infestation are crinkled leaves and white blotches and dashes on leaves of onions, peas, cucumbers, and melons	apply insecticide between leaves, making repeat applications; thrips grow in weeds and grass; mowing around crops keeps their numbers down

True Bugs. Although all insects are often called "bugs," true bugs, which include harlequin bugs, stinkbugs, and squash bugs, make up only part of one insect order called Hemiptera. This group does not have a larval stage; instead, the immature bugs look like tiny versions of the adults. Some species are beneficial and feed on other insect pests. True bugs have piercing-sucking mouthparts used to suck plant sap. They may also feed on fruit, causing spotting or blotching.

Harlequin bug

Pest	Description	Control
Harlequin bug	red-and-black bugs suck sap from cabbage, broccoli, and collards, turning leaves brown and causing plants to wilt	handpick adults early; to help prevent reinfestation, remove all plant debris as soon as vegetable is through producing
Squash bug	shield-shaped brown bugs attack squash, pumpkins, and cantaloupe; squash bugs inject substance into vines during feeding, causing plants to wilt; an infestation will kill plants	handpick adults early; to help prevent reinfestation, remove all plant debris as soon as vegetable is through producing
Stinkbug	brown or green bugs suck sap from stems and fruit; attack nearly all vegetables	handpick adults early; to help prevent reinfestation, remove all plant debris as soon as vegetable is through producing

Squash bug

Stinkbug

Other Pests

These are pests that do not fall into the major groups listed above but are likely to feed on your crops.

Pest	Description	Control
Leaf miner	larvae of flies, moths, or beetles feed inside leaves; most damaging to cabbage and other crops in which leaf is edible portion; causes yellowing or leaves to drop	difficult to control because miners are protected inside plant; tomatoes can withstand infestation of ¼ to ⅓ of foliage without significant decrease in yield; rotate crops to break life cycle
Nematode	microscopic eel-like worms live in soil and attack roots of okra, tomatoes, Southern peas, and other vegetables; cause poor growth, wilting, and yellowing foliage; infected roots may be stubby, galled, rough, black, discolored, or decayed; root knot nematodes, the most common, produce knots in roots of plants	difficult to control; plant resistant selections; plant ground cover of trap crop that attracts them, such as French marigold selections Tangerine, Petite Gold, Petite Harmony, Goldie, or Nemagold; let marigolds grow in garden at least 90 days, then discard; nematodes spread by infested soil that clings to pets, shoes, clothing, or tools; avoid using soil from infested areas
Slug and snail	slugs and snails feed at night on leafy greens and tender fruit; can strip young transplants of leaves overnight; worst in moist soils covered with mulch	to trap, sink plastic margarine tub into soil so lip is flush with ground, fill tub with 1 inch of beer, cut 2- to 3-inch hole in lid and put lid in place to keep pests from crawling out; sprinkle with lime or wood ashes to deter them

Slug

Plant Diseases

Three quarters of the diseases in a vegetable garden are caused by fungi. You can reduce the incidence of many of these diseases by instituting good garden practices and by planting selections that resist or tolerate the disease. When starting seedlings indoors, avoid damping-off, a fungus that rots young seedlings, by using sterile soil and seeds. Provide bright light, good air circulation, and enough moisture to keep soil damp but not soggy.

Blights. Blights are characterized by a sudden, rapid yellowing or browning of affected areas of leaves and fruit. Because blights spread so quickly, they need to be controlled early.

Disease	Description	Control
Gummy stem blight	leaves develop gray to brown dead areas and turn yellow and shrivel; affects cucumbers, melons, pumpkins, and squash	plant resistant selections; rotate crops; remove affected parts of the plant; avoid wetting foliage with water
Southern blight	plants die suddenly for no apparent reason; affects all vegetables; first sign is white, string-like growth at base of plant	plant resistant selections; keep mulch away from base of stem; make sure soil contains ample organic matter and nitrogen; avoid wetting foliage with water

Leaf Spots. Leaf spots are the most prevalent diseases. Many are not devastating, but a few can ruin your crop. Leaf spots are worst in wet seasons.

Disease	Description	Control
Anthracnose	small, dry, gray, yellow, or tan spots appear on foliage of beans, cucumbers, melons, peas, peppers, or tomatoes in humid weather; many types of fungi cause anthracnose; symptoms vary among plants	plant resistant selections; prune or remove diseased plants; water healthy plants with soaker hose to avoid wetting foliage
Cercospora	dark spots appear on leaves of beans, Southern peas, beets, and other vegetables; rarely kills plants	plant resistant selections

Anthracnose

Mildews. The fungus that causes a particular mildew is seen as a growth on the surface of the leaves that looks like mildew. This disease is worse in spring and fall.

Disease	Description	Control
Downy mildew	yellow areas or spots appear on upper surface of leaf, downy patches of white, gray, or violet-gray mold on underside; common in cool, humid weather; attacks cucumbers, melons, onions, mustard, lettuce, cauliflower, and spinach	plant resistant selections
Powdery mildew	white, dust-like growth on foliage; attacks green peas, melons, and cucumbers; stunts growth	plant resistant selections; remove affected plant parts; water in early morning with drip irrigation

Powdery mildew

Viruses and Bacteria. Viruses cause plants to become stunted and are most severe in late summer and early fall. One way to reduce viruses is to control sucking insects, such as aphids, that can spread the viruses from plant to plant. Viruses may also be found on seed, so be sure to obtain seeds from a reputable source or from plants that were not infected.

Bacteria can cause a variety of diseases that mimic leaf spots, rots, or blight.

Disease	Description	Control
Bacterial black rot	leaf edges turn yellow, veins darken; affects cabbage, cole crops, and sweet potatoes	buy disease-free plants and seed; rotate crops
Bacterial spot	small, dark, water-soaked spots on leaves	plant resistant selections
Bacterial wilt	leaves suddenly wilt and shrivel; affects cucumbers, squash, pumpkins, and honeydew	plant resistant selections
Bean mosaic virus	leaves curl up; fruit is deformed and matures late; attacks beans and peas	plant resistant selections; remove infected plants
Tobacco Mosaic Virus	leaves are mottled yellow and green and may be curled and stunted; badly infested plants die; attacks eggplant, tomatoes, peppers, and spinach	plant resistant selections; remove infected plants; wash hands after smoking or handling tobacco

Bacterial wilt

Wilts. Wilts are diseases that inhibit a plant's ability to absorb water; affected plants do not recover even after you water. Because wilts spread within the plant, they are impossible to control. The best way to avoid wilts is to plant selections that are resistant.

Disease	Description	Control
Fusarium wilt	lower leaves then higher parts of plant turn yellow and wilt; soilborne fungus affects tomatoes, melons, Southern peas, and beans	plant resistant selections; prune or remove diseased plants; water with soaker hose; rotate crops; provide good drainage
Verticillium wilt	fungus lives in soil during prolonged periods of cool weather; attacks eggplant and tomatoes; older leaves yellow and stems wilt	plant resistant selections; prune or remove diseased plants; water with soaker hose; rotate crops

Pseudo Diseases. Vegetables may develop problems that appear disease related but are actually due to environmental factors, such as the weather.

Disease	Description	Control
Blossom end rot	fruit develop round, sunken brown area on bottom, or blossom end; on ripe tomatoes, area usually turns black; also affects cucumbers, squash, melons, and peppers	plant resistant selections; keep soil evenly moist; use fertilizer that supplies calcium or lime; spray plants with Stop Rot, a calcium chloride solution, according to label directions

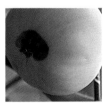

Blossom end rot

Index

Index

Special Thanks

Barbara Ball

Clemson University Extension Service in Cooperation with Federal Extension Service USDA, photographs, 123, stinkbug; 124, anthracnose

Department of Entomology, Oregon State University, Ken Gray Collection, photographs, 120, asparagus beetle; 122, onion thrip; 123, squash bug and slug

Thomas E. Eltzroth, photographs, 50; 55, bottom

National Garden Bureau, photographs, 54; 55, top; 103, bottom

Shepherd Ogden, photographs, 52, 74–77

PetoSeed

Progressive Farmer

Howard L. Puckett, photograph, 64, bottom

Barry Schilit, Weather Trends, Inc.

Southern Progress Corporation Library Staff